INTRODUCING THE
MISSIONAL
CHURCH

WHAT IT IS, WHY IT MATTERS, HOW TO BECOME ONE

ALAN J. ROXBURGH AND M. SCOTT BOREN
GENERAL EDITOR: MARK PRIDDY

BakerBooks

a division of Baker Publishing Group
Grand Rapids, Michigan

© 2009 by Alan J. Roxburgh and M. Scott Boren

Published by Baker Books
a division of Baker Publishing Group
P.O. Box 6287, Grand Rapids, MI 49516-6287
www.bakerbooks.com

Printed in the United States of America

Library of Congress Cataloging-in-Publication Data
Roxburgh, Alan J.
     Introducing the missional church : what it is, why it matters, how to become one /
Alan J. Roxburgh and M. Scott Boren ; general editor, Mark Priddy.
          p.   cm. — (Allelon missional series)
     Includes bibliographical references.
     ISBN 978-0-8010-7212-3 (pbk.)
     1. Mission of the church. 2. Missions—Theory. I. Boren, M. Scott. II. Priddy, Mark.
III. Title.
BV601.8.R688 2009
262′.7—dc22   2009028579

09   10   11   12   13   14   15   7   6   5   4   3   2   1

This book is more than the work of two authors, it has been written over a decade through interaction with ordinary men and women in local churches around the world. We dedicate this book to them—people in the United States, UK, Australia, Europe, New Zealand, Canada, South Africa. We are indebted to their passion for God and desire to see the church re-engage neighborhoods and communities with the imagination of the Spirit.

Contents

5

Contents

Series Preface

Allelon is a network of missional church leaders, schools, and para-church organizations that envisions, inspires, engages, resources, trains, and educates leaders for the church and its mission in our culture. Said simply, together we are a movement of missional leaders.

We have a particular burden for people involved in new forms of missional communities (sometimes called "emerging"), people starting new congregations within denominational systems, and people in existing congregations who are working toward missional identity and engagement. Our desire is to encourage, support, coach, and offer companionship for missional leaders as they discern new models of church capable of sustaining a living and faithful witness to the gospel in our contemporary world.

The word *allelon* is a common but overlooked Greek word that is reciprocal in nature. In the New Testament it is most often translated "one another." Christian faith is not an individual matter. Everything in the life of the church is done *allelon* for the sake of the world. A Christian community is defined by the *allelon* sayings in Scripture, a few of which include: love one another, pursue one another's good, and build up one another.

The overarching mission of Allelon is to educate and encourage the church, while learning from *one another*, so that we might become a people among whom God lives as sign, symbol, and foretaste of his redeeming love in neighborhoods and the whole of society. We seek to facilitate this reality within ordinary women and men who endeavor to participate in God's mission to reclaim and restore the whole of creation and to bear witness to the world of a new way of being human.

To accomplish this goal, Allelon has partnered with Baker Books and Baker Academic to produce resources that equip the church with the best thinking and practices on missional life. After years of interaction around the missional conversation, we continually get asked, "What is a missional church?" and then the follow-up question, "How do we become one?" This is the reason why we feel this book is especially important on this leg of the church's journey. Alan and Scott are trusted friends and colleagues who have poured their lives into this message that is based on both experience and research. You will find these words challenging and even somewhat unique. In fact, you may find their insights surprising; however, these are words you can trust to lead us forward as God's people into a new future.

Mark Priddy
CEO, Allelon International
Eagle, Idaho
www.allelon.org

Introduction

In 1974 a missionary returned home to his native England after more than thirty years in India. Seeing his own country after so many years away, he viewed it as an outsider with insider eyes and was shocked by what he observed. The Christian England he had left was gone; the depth of hopelessness he saw among the young was alarming. He realized that the West (the United Kingdom, Europe, and increasing portions of North America) was now itself a mission field. The once mission-sending nations of the West were in need of radical re-missionizing. This shock, with its awareness of the challenge to be addressed, became the focus of his work and writing for the next twenty-five years. The basic question he asked was about the nature of a missionary encounter with the modern West.

The man was Lesslie Newbigin. His work inspired the development of what came to be designated the Gospel and Our Culture Network that sprang up in the United Kingdom, New Zealand, and North America. The New Zealand group came to an end in the 1990s, and the movement in the United Kingdom has remained a relatively small, academic conversation. The North American Gospel and Our Culture Network had a somewhat different story.

In the late 1980s a group of church leaders and thinkers formed the Gospel and Our Culture Network in North America to ask basic questions about why and how churches had become so captive to individualism and consumerism. They wondered why churches had lost touch with the way the biblical texts spoke of God's mission in and for the world and why the central biblical theme of the kingdom of God had just about disappeared from the preaching and teaching of the churches.

Out of these conversations a team of authors collaborated to produce the book *Missional Church: A Vision for the Sending of the Church in North America*.[1] It touched a deep chord across North America so that by the beginning of the new millennium the missional conversation was the primary way church leaders talked about the challenges facing the church. While the book reframed the questions about being the church in North America at the end of the twentieth century, many local church leaders found it too abstract with too many concepts veiled in technical and academic language. Most of those who wrote *Missional Church* were academics teaching as theologians and missiologists in seminaries. Alan Roxburgh, one of the authors of that book as well as this one, remembers a conversation with a denominational leader about a year after the book's publication. His comments were telling: "I love the book. Its argument and ideas are the right ones. But few of my leaders will have any clue what it is about because the book is too technical and academic. If one of my pastors came into this office to ask for help in making his or her church a place that could engage its world, I couldn't give the pastor this book. There's nothing practical in it." He then turned to another section of his bookshelf and pulled down a thick workbook on how to make the church healthy. "I can give the pastor this because it tells how to do something. But your book just talks academic ideas." It was tough criticism to hear, but Alan understood what he meant.

Although part of the writing team, Alan had shifted from teaching in a seminary to pastoring a local church, so he had some sympathy with the denominational leader's plea for help. Many in Alan's church felt the missional conversation was a new program brought in by the new pastor, and they were his guinea pigs. Others were excited about the ideas but wondered what it all meant for existing programs and their identity as a church. Getting from the book's academic ideas to the down-to-earth practicalities of missional life looked like a big, big challenge.

When Alan was part of the team writing *Missional Church*, Scott Boren served on the staff of the church where Alan was pastor. Alan shared the concepts with the pastoral staff, and we discussed the implications for the way our church functioned. We had many of these conversations, which gave us an opportunity that few others at the time had to talk about the practical ways the missional church might play out. In our discussions we were looking for a plan that would make us a missional church. Being competent leaders, we thought we had a good plan for leading our church into a missional future. Little did we know we had simply embarked upon an unknown journey on which we would have to rethink from the ground up what it means to be God's people.

Since those days, both of us have moved on to other responsibilities working for different organizations. During that time we independently tested ideas, researched missional innovators, observed unexpected developments, and began to produce practical resources to help churches move into this missional vision. Three years ago an opportunity arose for us to work together again. It has allowed us to refine our communication about the missional church and get it out of the realm of theory and academics and into the everyday life of churches. We are now realizing the implications of what was initiated by Lesslie Newbigin more than thirty years ago. This book seeks to answer the question of how these important developments become accessible and usable for the whole church.

The book is divided into three parts. Part 1 addresses what it means to have a missional imagination that causes us to ask a different set of questions than is addressed in much of the material currently available on church strategy. With such an imagination, we discover the nature of a missional river to carry the church into the vast, uncharted missionary context of our time.

Part 2 identifies three missional conversations that generate understanding of what the missional church is and why it is so vital. Instead of a list of characteristics, traits, or programs of a missional church, we have observed that these three conversation topics shape the life of a missional people. They help us create ways of journeying together in a time and place where many of the habits of church life we had taken for granted no longer work. Although these occur in different ways in different churches, they serve as markers that help us discern what God is doing in a strange, new land.

Part 3 shares some key ways to enter the missional river, outlining the journey that lies ahead of local churches and church systems. The journey of a particular church cannot be prescribed in a book. Each is a unique story forming its own ways of being God's missionary people in its own neighborhoods and communities. Instead we propose a way of listening to the imagination the Spirit is giving ordinary people in local churches. This is where we discover the missional pathways the Spirit is birthing in our time. We want to emphasize that it's a movement of ordinary people in ordinary churches, because this is where the Spirit is at work gestating and birthing a new movement of God. The releasing of the missional imagination of God's people in the midst of the ordinary and everyday is far more powerful and transforming than importing a predetermined plan from the outside.

Let's see where the journey takes us.

Part 1

ONE MISSIONAL RIVER

1

Not All Who Wander Are Lost

Stories of a Church In Between

There once was a people who were neither significant nor exceptional nor privileged. In fact they did what most people of the time did: worked, married, raised children, celebrated, mourned, and carried out the basic stuff of life. You would not think them unique, because their dress, homes, and professions were much like that of everyone else. What was different about them, however, was their strange conviction that they had been chosen by God to be a special people, a journeying people who were forced to discover again and again what God wanted them to be doing in the world.

That community was what the Bible calls "the people of God," and their stories are captured in Abram's leaving of Ur, the wilderness wandering of the Israelites, the partial occupation of the Promised Land, and the Babylonian exile. We also have insight into their life through the stories of the early churches, partially told by Luke in his Gospel and the book of Acts. From these stories we see how God's people were sojourners, like their father Abraham, who sought a home like strangers in a foreign land, looking for a city with foundations, whose architect and builder is God (Heb. 11:9–10). At every stage in the biblical narratives is hope for a future reality toward which the people are moving. Being missional means we join this heritage, entering a journey without any road maps to discover what God is up to in our neighborhoods and communities. Before examining the shape of our journey, let's look at what this meant for the first Christians.

First-Century Wanderers

In some ways the church founded in Jerusalem after Pentecost failed to recognize the nature of the journey onto which the Spirit was calling them. These Christians immediately settled into a pattern they thought exemplified God's mission as they met at the temple as Jews had done for centuries, and they met in small settings as extended households with a sense of belonging and fellowship. They saw themselves as basically a Jewish movement that was the completion of God's people.

If this mind-set had remained, this Jesus-follower movement would have been little more than a branch of Judaism—not the Christian church. They had turned the teaching and life of Jesus into an improvement of the Judaism of the time instead of understanding it as a radical re-visioning that removed Jerusalem from the center. What transpired wasn't planned, strategized, or chosen: persecution forced many of the believers to flee their precious center in Jerusalem, and the Spirit broke the boundaries and shattered the assumptions these Christians had too quickly made about the location of God's future.

Then the boundary-breaking, assumption-challenging Spirit took some unknown Christians from Jerusalem north toward Antioch where they encountered Gentiles who had heard about Jesus and wanted to learn more. What happened next was outside the imagination of those early Christians and could not be controlled by the church in Jerusalem. As they spoke to the Gentiles about Jesus, the Holy Spirit fell upon them and a new kind of church was birthed in Antioch, comprised mostly of Gentiles.

Nobody expected this turn of events. This did not fit the plans and paradigms of the first followers of Jesus. The Spirit broke boundaries that were already defining what it meant to be Christian. The church was forced out of the box it had created and into a space it had never imagined and would never have entered by itself.

We might say, using our own categories, these first-century followers of Jesus were moved from a well-defined attractional way

[handwritten marginal note: Maybe too tinged w/ discontinuous w/ Judaism]

16

of doing church into a missional imagination of being the church in the world. The church in Jerusalem was an attractional model of church life because it sought to draw people into the center of a predetermined understanding of what it meant to be God's people. It was a Jerusalem-centered movement shaped by the assumptions of Judaism. They saw Jesus as the Jewish Messiah who had come to fulfill the promises for the Jewish people. They were not able to grasp the extent to which Jesus's mission was greater than the imagination that had shaped them to that point. They could not comprehend that the Spirit was about to take them beyond their attractional center and lead them to wander on a mission they did not fully understand.

None of this makes those early believers failures, nor does it render useless what they sought to achieve in Jerusalem. We simply want to recognize that the Spirit is always shaping something far greater than we imagine and that there is a natural tendency to try to fit the work of the Spirit into old familiar patterns. We believe something similar is happening in the life of the church in North America; a stirring is taking place; the Spirit is up to something where we least expect the presence of God to break out. People are tiring of the attractional pattern as the primary focus of their churches; they are hungering for a different journey.

Attractional and Missional

"If you build it, they will come." This imagination shaped Kevin Costner's character in the movie *Field of Dreams*. And it is still the dominant imagination of the church, whether traditional, contemporary, seeker, or emergent. Figure 1 illustrates how it can be pictured.

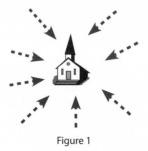

Figure 1

17

The assumption of the attractional imagination is that average people outside the church are looking for a church and know they should belong to one, and therefore, church leaders should create the most attractive attractional church possible. The mission, then, is to get people to attend. This story is still repeated over and over again across North America. It's not that we shouldn't be attractive for those looking for a church to attend; it's that this has become the primary focus of churches, and as a result they miss what the Spirit is up to in the world.

It's an old story: A congregation recognizes its neighborhood has changed dramatically. The leadership senses something has shifted, and they want to reach out to the new realities of their context. They upgrade the building to make it more attractive to outsiders, putting in new carpet, giving the place a paint job, and hanging religious art on the walls. Then they change the Sunday service: alongside the *traditional* service at 11:00 a.m., they now offer a new *contemporary* service at 9:30 with a worship band, PowerPoint slides for the worship lyrics, and even a bit of drama. The sermons shift from expositional preaching to themes like "How the Bible Helps to Make Your Life Work." They hire a marketing consultant to develop new brochures to communicate the kind of people they are as a church and why others would want to join them. Finally, they decide to hire a new youth and children's worker who provides high-quality programs.

Alan was a pastor in the Pacific Northwest. Before his arrival, the church had created a program called "Walk to Bethlehem." Each year by mid-November the church building was transformed as rooms were turned into ten or more different sets depicting the story of the birth of Jesus. It was an amazing undertaking done with exceptional quality and ability. Without any exaggeration, thousands of people from the community came during the four days of performances. In a thirty-minute walk they moved through each of the scenes, stopping to watch people in costume act out a biblical event. At the end of the program people were given beautifully designed cards inviting them to the church's series of Christmas services. Attractional.

The attractional way of doing church is not limited to new innovations. Scott grew up in a small, rural Southern Baptist church in North Texas. On Sunday afternoons church members did what they called *visitation*. This was a time when we visited either people who were prospects for attending church or people who had not been to church in a while. Later, as a youth intern in a large Baptist church in Houston, Scott loaded up the car with the faithful youth on Tuesday nights and visited homes of other young people, telling them about the upcoming events. The hope was to generate some interest in the church so that more people would come.

Attractional churches come in many different forms: they can be very traditional or very innovative; they can be small or large; the preaching can be Bible centered or liturgy driven. The common theme is that *church* is about an event (usually the Sunday morning services) and about getting people to attend that event. Those who come to this event expect certain people will provide *spiritual goods and services* that will help them live better lives. From the perspective of the average church attendee, church plays a specific and limited role of speaking to their *spiritual* life, and it has little to nothing to do with how they live with their families or at their workplaces. If the measure of church success is how many people come to an event, the church must meet the expectations of providing excellent spiritual goods and services to attract people.

But what happens when people don't respond to this attractional marketing anymore? What do we do when we realize that no matter how good we build it, they aren't coming? Worse still, what happens when even the successful megachurches realize that their success is just a veneer that may have addressed the reactive needs of a specific generation but has little connection with the emerging generations? As one local pastor confessed, "All we're doing is putting on a better show for Christians who move from their small church to our big church with all the programs and pizzazz. I'm not sure that's how I want to spend the rest of my life."

You may be reading this thinking, *What's wrong with getting people to come to church meetings?* You may be asking, *Why are you attacking what the church has done for generations?* Let us be clear: we do not intend to attack or to denigrate being attractive in what a church does. No one should plan a worship event or a program unless it's attractive. Neither of us would be content to lead a church that intentionally repels people because we have some ideal vision of *being missional.* There is nothing wrong or bad about attracting people to attend the various meetings that a church holds. We

19

are not advocating an either/or imagination that demands that we move from attractional to missional. That would be a sign of poor leadership. If we are good leaders in a church that is good at what it does, then we will attract people, and that is good. We are simply saying that the attractional pattern is not the goal or the primary call of the church.

The Missional Church Is Not about the Church

We need an alternative imagination to the attractional in order to understand the missional church. This imagination starts with a paradoxical statement that often leaves people confused: A missional imagination is not about the church; it's not about how to make the church better, how to get more people to come to church, or how to turn a dying church around. It's not about getting the church back to cultural respectability in a time when it has been marginalized. All of these are good things, but they aren't the focus of a missional imagination.

God is up to something in the world that is bigger than the church even though the church is called to be sign, witness, and foretaste of God's purposes in the world. The Spirit is calling the church on a journey outside of itself and its internal focus. Rowan Williams, archbishop of Canterbury, summarizes this imagination in this way: "It is not the church of God that has a mission. It's the God of mission that has a church." He is saying God is at work in the world to redeem creation, and God invites us to participate in this mission. God is not interested in getting more and more people into the institution of the church. Instead the church is to be God's hands and feet in accomplishing God's mission. This imagination turns most of our church practices on their head. It invites us to turn toward our neighborhoods and communities, listening first to what is happening among people and learning to ask different questions about what God is up to in the neighborhood. Rather than the primary question being, "How do we attract people to what we are doing?" it becomes, "What is God up to in this neighborhood?" and "What are the ways we need to change in order to engage the people in our community who no longer consider church a part of their lives?" This is what a missional imagination is about.

To be quite honest, the idea that the predominant form of attractional church life is faulty is not new or novel. Over the past forty years there has been a litany of books that have raised the concern about the attractional church where spiritual things happen in spiritual buildings at spiritual times led by spiritual people. There is wide-scale agreement that this falls short of God's purposes. As an alternative to the attractional, some take up a contrarian stance. They become anti-building, anti-clergy, anti-denomination, anti-megachurch, anti-tradition, and anti-structure. They point fingers at what is now in place and tear it down. Many are stuck on the negative, and they know how to write blogs that deconstruct and talk about what is wrong. Who doesn't know how to do that? There's nothing creative about it, even if the media is used well. Others move past the negative by elevating an ideal or dream of what the church should be. This is understandable, but it is not helpful. As counterintuitive as it may sound, we don't cultivate a missional imagination by setting up some ideal type of the church or telling people what we should be. There are different forms of these dreams. They often come in some form of *getting back to New Testament patterns* or describing some point in the church's history that we need to recover. Some use quite strange, almost nonsensical language about how the church must become deinstitutionalized (we actually haven't come across any human system that isn't institutionalized in one form or another) and that it needs to return to a preinstitutionalized state of organic life. None of this is helpful, because it fails to recognize where the Spirit is actually at work in shaping a new imagination.

Show Me a Model

When people engage the missional church conversation, one of the first questions they ask is, "Can you show me a missional church model?" They assume that the missional church is following the pattern about an ideal church and providing a model to emulate. They want to know if there is a church that is doing this successfully and has worked out all the unknowns and kinks. These are understandable questions, but they are only relevant in a stable and predictable church world in which there was continuity over time and models were easy to find. We don't live in that world anymore. While we will tell stories about churches on God's mission, we can't point to a model that can be copied or emulated. Once we offer a model of missional church, the focus of our imagination turns to internal questions about how to do missional church correctly or how we can measure ourselves against this predetermined model. This would be to entirely miss what missional church is about.

Instead we need to see ourselves being called out of the comfort and security of attractional church life onto a journey like Abram leaving Ur of the Chaldees; we are moving into a strange land without maps to guide us on our way to a land God will show us. We are like those early Christians after the church at Antioch was birthed by the Spirit. We know something has shifted, but no one has the formula; it's confusing and filled with friction as we try to figure out the next steps.

When we teach seminars on this topic, we wonder if it would be helpful to hang two signs so that no one misses this point:

Beware of formulas for creating missional churches!

and

Beware of missional church models!

When we heed this warning, we launch out upon a vast river where we have never been before; we move into a place where we are guided by the Spirit in the formation of a church that steps outside the bounds of being merely attractional. The local churches the Spirit will shape on these unknown waters will come in many different forms: new, developing churches and old, traditional congregations; large, small, and medium churches; denominationally connected and independent churches. There isn't one specific form, predictable pattern, or predetermined model. On these new waters we become pioneers who are creating new maps shaped in, with, and for the contexts and communities into which we have been called. Here we will learn to experiment and test ideas. Some will work; others will fail. Through trial and error we will imagine new ways of being Jesus's people.

Why Not a Formula or Blueprint?

In times of significant change or high anxiety, it is normal for us to instinctively turn to people we view as experts. This is why we often find security in authors and church consultants who claim they have the answers to this new space and can provide plans for success. Just as there are a multitude of attractional models, we assume there must be a list of missional models we can easily replicate. A missional way of life, however, calls us away from answers with formulas and blueprints. It is an invitation to move out of our comfort zones.

Too often we have taken Luke's account of the early church as if it were a blueprint presenting the pattern for church life for all times and all places. We read it idealistically as the *pure* beginnings of the church that we should copy today. Some, for example, use it to support the notion of a large and small group structure (which is like going to the Bible to show that because some prophets in the Old Testament drove chariots, we can drive automobiles). Because the Jerusalem church met in the temple courts and from house to house, they conclude this pattern of meeting is the key reason for having large and small group gatherings today. Strange reasoning, but nevertheless, this is the level at which many believe the Bible gives us patterns and models for all times and all places. All human groups meet in small and large groups. It has nothing to do with a biblical pattern and everything to do with how humans meet together.

On the other hand, some point to the same passage and argue that the large meeting was actually not a consistent pattern in the life of the early church and that the house church was the only form of meeting. They conclude that the only *biblical* model for being the church is meeting in house churches, even proposing that all other forms of church meeting are actually pagan in origin. All of this goes to the basic flaw of assuming the New Testament is a template against which we measure all our structures and organizational forms so that some forms are more biblical than others. A moment of reflection reveals how silly all this is, but we often have a deeply embedded belief in blueprints that, once we have figured them out, give us the formula for getting everything right. But that wasn't Abram's experience, and it's far from the experiences of most of the characters and communities we encounter in Scripture. Most of the time they were being compelled to risk journeying with this God who called them out of their comfort zones, and they had to figure it out along the way.

We want to challenge three perspectives here. First, we are challenging the elevation of any model as *the* way to do church. The addiction to mimicry so easily entraps church leaders. The new way of doing church or the next great model for church life is always on the horizon. Cell church, megachurch, seeker church, purpose-driven church, house church, externally focused church, multisite church, equipping church, emerging church, simple church—all point to models, and someone is happy to provide us with resources to help pull off these models.

Second, we challenge arguments that the Bible reveals a *missional secret or formula* that provides twenty-first-century Christians with a magic pill for entering missional life. This never happened to figures in Scripture; why should it now be true for us?

Third, we are challenging the idea that there is some point in the history of the church that provides us with just the right pattern and formula for creating missional churches—such as the Celtic missionaries of the fifth and sixth centuries or what happened in China after the Christian missionaries were expelled. We don't live in those times and societies. For example, during the twentieth century Christians in China were persecuted, and the Chinese were steeped in communist philosophy. This kind of social context shaped new experiments that no one could have predicted at the time and that can't be simply duplicated or applied to a late-modern Western context in which democratic liberalism has reigned for three hundred years. No matter what era one chooses, there will always be much to learn and wisdom to be gained from listening to the stories of the churches in those times, but we cannot turn to them to find formulas and templates for our time. Just as God called the Celtic missionaries of Northumbria into risky, unknown journeys and the Christians of China into places they did not want to go and could not plan for, so we are being called into a new time of missional life. We are going to learn and discern how to be the church as we go.

Skilled Navigators

When Alan and Scott were serving in the same church in Vancouver, a couple joined the church who had recently immigrated from South Africa. Their journey was unusual. They had crossed the ocean in a twenty-foot sailboat and entered North America through a port in North Carolina. When they left South Africa, they knew where they wanted to go, but the path for getting there was less than predictable. Sailing any distance never occurs in a straight line; instead it involves tacking back and forth while moving toward the intended destination but never actually sailing directly at it. When you factor in the unpredictability of the winds, the currents of the waters, and storms, we cannot imagine what it would have taken to sail from South Africa to North Carolina.

Those on the missional journey are wanderers, and we need to develop skills of reading the winds of the Spirit, testing the waters of the culture, and running with the currents of God's call so that we are not lost on the journey. To some it might look like we are lost when we cannot point to a model that can be easily applied anywhere. Instead we are participants on a journey in which we have to learn from one another as we move toward becoming God's missional people.

All of this might feel about as solid as Jell-O. But it is the reality of the missional journey. In the following chapters we will get much more concrete about what this means, but if you choose to ignore this point about being on a journey without blueprints, you will not understand what we are really saying in the coming chapters. At the heart of this discussion is the need for us to let go of our desire to be in control of either the church or the place in which we find ourselves.

If You Have Read This Chapter

If you have made it to this point, you are part of the conversation. Welcome! You may not agree with what we have written, you may be looking for a model, or you may be happy with the result of the model you are currently using. If the adventure of missional church is about letting go of our need to control outcomes and manage people, or if it is about this Abram-like journey into a new space, then this chapter is a first step on the journey.

You will have questions. There will be things you have to go back and think about. You will want to have conversations with others. Even if you disagree with some or all of what you read here, we encourage you to stick with the journey a little longer. God is up to something bigger than any of *our* ways; he is beyond all of our models, but the Spirit is in the midst of our questions. The following chapters aim to generate a conversation about this journey by contrasting *missional* with *attractional* ways of church life and raising questions about too easily accepting the new formulas and templates that promise quick results for being missional. The places where we feel like we have little control and don't know what is going to happen are exactly the places where God's future breaks forth. In 1998 the World Council of Churches concluded their assembly with words that can point us forward:

> We are challenged by the vision of a church that will reach out to everyone, sharing, caring, proclaiming the good news of God's redemption, a sign of the kingdom and a servant of the world.
>
> We are challenged by a vision of a church, the people of God on the way together, confronting all divisions of race, gender, age or culture striving to realize justice and peace upholding the integrity of creation.
>
> We journey together as a people of prayer. In the midst of confusion and loss of identity, we discern signs of God's purpose being fulfilled and expect the coming of God's reign.
>
> We expect the healing of human community, the wholeness of God's entire creation.[1]

2

Just Give Me a Definition

Why Missional Church *Is So Hard to Define*

Saul of Tarsus spent enough time in Jerusalem watching and listening to this new sect of people—followers of Jesus—to know quite well what their definitions and ideas were. He was in the crowd when Stephen addressed the leaders of Jerusalem, and he was in on the talk in the city about the claims that Jesus was the fulfillment of God's promises. Information and definitions were not the issue; what Saul needed was a radical transformation of his imagination—of the way in which he saw the world. He knew the definitions of Jesus and his disciples, but he filtered them through his own way of seeing the world. As a result he came up in a very different place from the followers of Jesus. As far as Saul was concerned, these people were dangerously wrong and had to be put in prison to silence them. Definitions, then, aren't necessarily going to solve the problem of understanding what *missional* means. Something else needs to happen.

Saul's imagination—his way of seeing the world—had to be transformed. An illustration of this problem can be seen in the ways we approach the idea of the attractional church. Generally we find it quite easy to explain what it means. We talk about the needs of seekers and the importance of contemporary worship with relational preaching, and most people will understand what *attractional* means. It's like a magnet—it attracts the iron filings toward it; there's a pull that draws them together. We can use more familiar words and illustrations to make sense of a word and then declare, "I get it!" A well-known image that illustrates this concept is shown here. Depending on your perspective, you will see either a vase or the silhouette of two faces.

Figure 2

The power of the image we see is that it then becomes really hard to see anything other than what we are predisposed to see. This is why new ideas or new ways of doing things are initially so hard to accept; we take the way we see the world and apply it to the new ideas. We could be given a lot of definitions about vases and faces, but that won't really help us *see* either. Something more is needed. Our point: it simply takes time to get inside a new idea, and definitions won't do it for us. In order to see what is going on, we need something more than a definition.

Words Get in the Way

People often get frustrated with this talk of a *missional imagination*. They ask why we can't just come up with a simple definition. It should, after all, be easy to define *missional church*, because it's made up of two very familiar and simple words: *mission* and *church*. If those words are so familiar, why is it that when we put the two together we have a different entity that does not easily fit into our standard definitions?

Ask any group about the meaning of the word *mission* and you'll discover it's so well understood that people come up with a long list of definitions, such as:

- people going overseas as foreign missionaries
- people working in an inner city
- a new church start-up in an ethnically diverse area
- young people and adults going for a short-term mission experience
- a campaign to raise funds for mission work
- a category in a church budget of money given for work outside the church
- a statement on the front of the Sunday bulletin that tells why we exist as a church

In each of these definitions, *mission* is defined as something the church does as part of its life and programs. When foreign missionaries return home, for example, and talk about what God is doing in another country, people automatically know they are talking about *missions*. In all of these responses, *mission* refers to what happens *outside* the church for other people or groups. For the sake of simplicity we call this a *missionary imagination* (see figure 3).

Similarly, the word *church* is one with which most people are familiar. They have an image or idea in their head of what it means that has been given to them by their culture. We have used this word in a certain way so much that no abstract definition is required to have a shared understanding. People will tell you very quickly that the word *church* describes the place where one goes to:

- worship
- receive training in Christian life
- have one's child baptized
- bury someone
- find community with other Christians
- receive care and nurture from one another and from professional pastors
- equip one another in service and ministry

When we use the word *church*, we get a picture in our imagination that depicts what transpires in or through a building for those who *stereotype :*

are inside the world of church life. In short, *church* is for insiders while *mission* is for outsiders. This is a common misperception, and in most cases the confusion arises because we try to combine the *attractional imagination* with the *missionary imagination* (see figure 3).

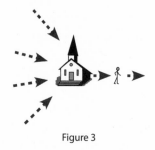

Figure 3

The words *mission* and *church* are, therefore, used together to define a church that attracts, worships, equips, and then sends. And of course the sending has the purpose of bringing back more people to the attractional event. Because of this, people conclude that being missional is not much different from what they have been doing. The majority of the people attend church, and a few individuals do missions. They get confused and jump to questions about these definitions, such as the following:

- Is *missional church* different from *missions*? If so, how is it different?
- Is *missional church* different from *evangelism*? In what ways is it different?
- Is the missional church some new fad like so many others that pass through the church?
- Do we really need a new set of words that no one understands?

The word *missional* was introduced in 1998 because the definitions of *mission* and *church* presented above are misleading and wrong. Adding the *al* to the end of *mission*, however, creates a new meaning we don't immediately see or understand. The word invites us to stop, check our assumptions, and ask if there might be a different way of being the church.

30

Missional Church Definitions

The team who wrote *Missional Church* introduced the word *missional* as an invitation for people to consider a new way of being the church. It was intended to create a space in which we could get a new imagination for what God wants to do in and through the church. That was over ten years ago, and today there is an extreme problem: *missional church* has become a label used to describe practically everything a church does. For the sake of clarity and at the risk of being repetitious, we feel we need to point out some of the common definitions for *missional church* that are different from what we want to describe in this book.

Our intention is not to undermine how people define these words or to claim we own *the* way of using missional language; we just want to be clear about what we believe is at stake. Therefore we will lay out eight trends in the missional conversation that illustrate what we do *not* mean when talking about *missional church*.

1. *Missional church* is not a label to describe churches that emphasize cross-cultural missions. While cross-cultural missions are important, the missional church conversation is not about *missions* as traditionally understood. The confusion arises from the fact that many churches that we would call missional are doing significant work in cross-cultural missions. Instead of relying on traditional denominational institutions to reach people groups, they are directly engaging these people by sending missionaries and partnering with local leaders in cross-cultural settings. But this is a modified version of a traditional perspective on missions. The *missional church* conversation can overlap with this new way of doing missions, but it does not equate it.

2. *Missional church* is not a label used to describe churches that are using outreach programs to be *externally focused*. Because the term *missional* means "being sent," people assume that the missional church is focused on outreach. While it is true that missional churches are entering and indwelling their neighborhoods and communities incarnationally, their focus is not on establishing *programs* to minister to people *outside* the church.

31

The church has long used this language of inside/outside that divides its life into internally and externally focused segments. The assumption is that the way *insiders* minister to *outsiders* is by doing something for the outsiders through programs or mission. We believe this keeps churches in a mode of being program-driven and treating people as objects that we attempt to draw inside the church. Building programs based on this inside/outside imagination establishes an us/them mentality. On the missional church journey we want to *pitch our tent* beside the people in our neighborhoods and communities as Jesus did (see John 1:1–14), not as a program but as a way of being the church. We want to enter these places in order to discern and discover how the Spirit will have us shape our lives as God's people. This is not about externally focused programs but about a radically different way of being church.

3. *Missional church* is not another label for church growth and church effectiveness. In the 1980s and 1990s, books abounded on this subject, and all the talk was about how to grow a church. And many churches grew: there are more "very large" churches (over 1,000 people) now than ever before in the history of the church. Most of these churches grew through transfers. They happened to develop more attractional religious goods and services for attendees. Being missional is not about getting people to come to a building, although more often than not missional churches will have buildings and corporate gatherings. But the focus and energy of a missional church is not church growth and counting noses at church events.

4. *Missional church* is not a label for churches that are effective at evangelism. While we don't want to diminish the importance of individuals choosing to trust Jesus as Lord, the common perspective of evangelism can lead people to misapply what it means to be missional. Missional churches do relate to non-Christians and invite them to enter the kingdom of God, but a reductionistic view of salvation limited to a private, individualistic conversion falls far short of being missional.

5. *Missional church* is not a label to describe churches that have developed a clear mission statement with a vision and purpose for their existence. Vision and mission statements and finding

32

the next way that provides a niche for a church in the spiritual marketplace misses the point of being missional. Missional churches are not missional because they have a mission statement or a clear definition of its purpose. There is nothing wrong with having these things, but that is not what we mean by *missional*.

6. *Missional church* is not a way of turning around ineffective and outdated church forms so that they can display relevance in the wider culture. North America is full of churches that are still structured around patterns developed in the 1950s or earlier. Some have found ways of getting unstuck and becoming successful. But missional churches move beyond relevance and concern themselves with how they are engaging and relating to the surrounding culture in everyday life.

7. *Missional church* is not a label that points to a primitive or ancient way of being the church. There are many who talk of an ideal era (usually the first three hundred years of church life) and call for the church to return to the practices of that period. The blame is usually laid at the feet of Emperor Constantine and the marriage between the church and society that he created. It is as if they are saying, "If only he had not declared himself a Christian, we would not be in this pickle." The reality is that there is no ideal way we should try to discover or recover from the past. The early church, as well as the church at a variety of points in history, was far from ideal. We don't live in first-century Eurasia. We don't get to live in an era previous to Constantine. This is our time and no other. We are on the other side of Christendom, and we are called by the Spirit to imagine and shape forms of being church that address our time and place. We must do this with a full sense of the history of the church but also with the clear understanding that there is no ideal, perfect, or right era in the past for us to copy.

8. *Missional* is not a label describing new formats of church that reach people who have no interest in traditional churches. Many churches carry the label of emergent, creative, liquid, simple, or postmodern, but they are simply attractional churches in a different form. Candles, couches, the arts, labyrinths, or dialogical preaching are all creative forms of church that are

being embraced in nontraditional church settings, but they don't necessarily form missional life. Being missional is more than being postmodern attractional.

In many cases *missional* is misunderstood to be simply a new language to describe things church leaders have already been saying and the church has been doing for quite a while. This makes people suspicious of missional language, causing them to assume it's just another trendy word. So even with clear and precise definitions, we are still seeing the missional conversation misused and turned into new language for existing forms of church. This can result in people investing lots of energy into missional models only to be disappointed not too far down the road because they have been taken on a path that holds little promise of joining with the Spirit who makes all things new.

Why Definitions Mislead

In Mark 1:14–15 we read, "After John was put in prison, Jesus went into Galilee proclaiming the good news of God. 'The time has come,' he said. 'The kingdom of God is near. Repent and believe the good news!'" This is a pivotal announcement of Jesus's purpose. In modern language, it is like an inaugural address; it is Jesus's mission statement. The kingdom of God is a *big* deal in the Old Testament. It is at the heart of all that God promises and all that is expected in the Scriptures. We can't overstate the importance and centrality of the kingdom in the minds and hearts of the people at that time. Here at the beginning of his Gospel, Mark states unequivocally that Jesus declares himself bearer and fulfillment of the kingdom. If we are to understand Jesus properly, we have to make sure we have a very clear, unambiguous understanding of the kingdom. If we don't get the kingdom right, we won't get Jesus right. It's that simple.

Just before the beginning of a daylong presentation with leaders of a mid-America mainline church, a tall, elegant, gray-haired man introduced himself to Alan. He was the recently retired CEO of a major global corporation. After exchanging pleasantries, he looked Alan in the eyes and said with a pleasant but firm voice: "I'm here on

34

the recommendation of others in this church, but I'm suspicious of these newfangled words you experts keep bringing into the church. So unless you can give me a good definition of *missional* before the end of the morning, I won't be convinced and I'll go home!" Alan thanked the man for coming and for his frank sentiments.

After some introductory material, Alan divided the room into groups of five to seven and gave them a series of texts out of the Gospels in which Jesus spoke of the kingdom of God.[1] He asked the groups to spend the next ten minutes with these texts and come up with a simple, clear definition of the kingdom of God. When they came back together, each group was asked to write their definition on a sheet of newsprint hung on the wall. Here is a sample of what one of the groups produced:

> The kingdom of God is when God's new future breaks into the present to change the ways people think about the world; it is when things happen that make it clear that everything must change because now God is doing what he promised he would always do.

As each of the definitions went up on the wall, you could hear the mumbling across the room as people conferred with one another. Finally, someone stood up and said: "You can't do it! You can't write a definition based on these texts—it's all coming out in abstract terms of propositions. But that's not what is going on in these texts. It's not possible to write a definition in the way we want to have definitions." People sensed something going on in these texts that they hadn't expected. How do you turn a story about a woman sweeping a room and finding a dime into a definition of the kingdom of God? How do you do that with a man plowing a field and finding a box, then going to sell everything he has to buy the field and get the box? How do you write a definition of the kingdom when Jesus tells us it's about mustard seeds and vineyards and cheating servants?

Alan asked, "What does it mean that the kingdom of God is so central to the message of Jesus but we can't define it?" As people wrestled with this new reality, he turned to the skeptical CEO and said, "Until you can give me a definition of the kingdom of God, I can't give you a definition of missional." The CEO smiled back and stayed the day.

People ask for definitions of missional church, assuming that if they first define the meaning then they can develop tactics and strategies to make it real. They believe that a definition must precede implementation. From this perspective the lack of a clear definition is the result of one of three things: (1) we don't have enough information; (2) the person speaking doesn't know what he is talking about; or (3) it's not real. Of course frustration is a natural result when a clear and distinct definition of missional church is not available.

How Definitions Work

Definitions are tricky. It's actually more difficult to come up with a clear, simple definition of something than we might imagine. When people in modern Western culture ask for definitions, we have a specific sense of what we want. A dictionary definition provides a simple, clear, concise three- or four-sentence statement capturing what something means. At one level or another, we all know that there are different ways of understanding and seeing the world, but we usually operate as if the way we have learned to see the world is normative for all people and all times. It is as if there is in each of us an assumption that the way we experience and interpret the world has always been that way. A normal expectation of a modern Western person is that everyone reads the world in much the same way we do. If we thought about this assumption for a moment, we would agree that it is wrong. But this is the way most of us have operated in the modern world. As a result we look for and expect clear, precise definitions for everything because our culture has shaped us to see the world this way.

But this is not the way most of the world has approached reality throughout history. Old Testament scholar Walter Brueggemann, for example, says this about the Hebrew text of the Old Testament:

> This text, in its very utterance, in its ways of putting things, is completely unfamiliar to us. The utterance of the primitive God of Scripture is an utterance that is in an unfamiliar mode. Let me say what I mean.
>
> Hebrew, even for those who know it much better than I do, is endlessly imprecise and unclear. It lacks the connecting words; it

denotes rather than connotes; it points and opens and suggests, but it does not conclude or define. That means it is a wondrous vehicle for what is suggested but hidden, what is filled with imprecision and inference and innuendo, a vehicle for contradiction, hyperbole, incongruity, disputation. Now the reason this may be important is that in a society of technological control and precision, we are seduced into thinking that if we know the codes, we can pin down all meaning, get all mysteries right and have our own way, without surprise, without deception, without amazement . . . without anything that signals mystery or risk.[2]

In the biblical imagination, dictionary definitions as we know them are not the norm. There is a different way of reading the world here. Like the three children in C. S. Lewis's story *The Lion, the Witch and the Wardrobe*, understanding the imagination at work in the Bible is something like going through a wardrobe into another world that many can't see and don't believe exists. Entering the missional conversation is more like going through the wardrobe than like getting the right definition. This is because there is this big difference between how we see our world in the modern period and the way Jesus saw the world when he told the stories about the kingdom of God. Let's explore this a little more to see if we can push ourselves a bit farther into the wardrobe or even into that other world.

As we pointed out, Jesus entered Galilee "proclaiming the good news of God. 'The time has come,' he said. 'The kingdom of God is near. Repent and believe the good news!'" (Mark 1:14–15). Jesus's inaugural announcement points to the centrality of the kingdom. But

Figure 4

how does Jesus describe and explain the kingdom? Given Bruegge-mann's description, Jesus's explanation was more like the diagram in figure 4.

The way Jesus spoke of the kingdom has a characteristic form. He begins with expressions like: "the kingdom of God is as if . . ." "the kingdom can be compared to . . ." "the kingdom of heaven is like. . . ." The kingdom is explained in metaphors, similes, images, and pictures. It is impossible to put all the images into one simple, rational definition for a dictionary. You can't codify these descriptions or contain them in a neat box. Jesus's words point, open, and suggest rather than conclude or define. This idea of the kingdom of God is filled with imprecision that can't be pinned down; it invites us to risk entering a world we may not be able to control or manipulate for our own needs (like going through the wardrobe into Narnia). This may be frustrating; it may create consternation in those demanding precision; but it invites us to risk having our imaginations invaded by the God who is *endlessly elusive*.[3] These descriptions of the kingdom (most of the Bible is like this) are not like our modern imagination, whereby we want everything clear, precise, and packaged into simple, abstract ideas we can control and manage as illustrated in figure 5.

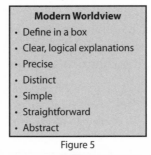

Figure 5

The implications for the missional conversation are clear. We have to become willing (like little children) to enter the strange world of the Bible. Unless we learn to do this, we will continue to read Scripture as a book filled with clear, simple definitions. The thing about definitions is that we use them to provide clarity that, in turn, has the potential of giving us control over our world. Definitions can be used to design strategies and implement plans that leave us in control, which is precisely what the God of Scriptures will not let us do. As we become willing to enter a new way of reading Scripture, we discover that the meaning of *missional* is more like the kingdom of God than any dictionary definition.

A Missional River

Scripture does not so much define reality as invite us onto a journey in which we discover the world God is creating. This can make us restless and confused. If we persist on this journey into the strange world of the Bible, it will form our imaginations in radically new ways; it will change how we see the world. This happened to the Hebrew people when they were called out of Egypt. They embarked on a journey for which they had little preparation and about which they could not have imagined while inside Egypt. Its meaning and shape had to be discovered along the way. They may have thought it would be a simple matter of tracing a well-traveled line on a map and getting to the Promised Land, but God had different things in mind. In the desert God shaped a people with an imagination that couldn't be taught or defined in Egypt. What might be involved in a change of imagination for us in order to get inside the missional conversation?

It's as though missional life is discovered out on a wide, wild river. How do we learn to navigate the river as it twists and turns and widens out into spaces where we have never been before? First we need to understand the nature of this river. It has been shaped by the confluence of three powerful currents we call *mystery*, *memory*, and *mission*.

Entering the missional waters is not about strategies or models; it is about working with the currents that shape our imagination of what God is doing in this world. Table 1 introduces and summarizes each current.

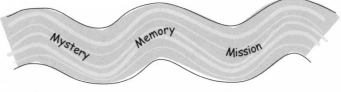

Figure 6

Table 1

Missional Imagination

Old Testament	New Testament
ISRAEL is a gift of God's originating mercy and grace and exists only because of God's resolve. God's action toward Israel can be summarized under three headings: Mystery, Memory, and Mission.	The CHURCH is a gift of God's new creation in the life, death, and resurrection of Jesus Christ. God's action in the church can be summarized under three headings: Mystery, Memory, and Mission.
MYSTERY Why this people out of all the people of the world? The only explanation is in God's sovereign choosing (election). Israel does not exist because of an act of history (i.e., circumstances or events). It was not chance that formed Israel; it was God's action. Israel is not the result of human preferences, and it is not the creation of some individual genius or group choice. Israel is the locus of God's presence, work, and power in the world.	MYSTERY Why this people out of all the people of the world? The only explanation is in God's sovereign choosing (election). The church is not an act of history—the chance result of events—which would also mean it could cease to have any place in history if circumstances changed. The church is not a human creation formed by the plans and actions of men and women. Indeed, the stories in the book of Acts state that the church emerged despite the people involved. The church is the locus of God's presence in Jesus Christ for the sake of the world (see Eph. 1:20).
MEMORY Israel exists only on the basis of a memory that lives at the core of her identity: "My father was a wandering Aramean" (Deut. 26:5). This memory and its specific story is the basis of a covenant agreement between people and God. Without this memory there is no agreement. It is by this memory that Israel knows herself as unavoidably a distinct people in all the world—they belong to the God of this memory, and that makes all the difference.	MEMORY The church exists on the basis of a specific story and memory rooted in the narratives about Jesus Christ. The church's life is rooted in a new covenant as God's new creation. But this new covenant is only available through the ongoing memory of one particular story. Memory forms a distinct people who are a parallel culture in the midst of all cultures. They cannot be the religious pillars for any nation.
MISSION Israel is called into life for the sake of the world. She is not to exist for herself. Israel lives as a sign and foretaste of what God will do for the whole creation. She is to be an alternative society for the sake of the world as a demonstration of where God is taking the whole creation.	MISSION The church is called into existence for the sake of the world. The church is to be the sign, witness, and foretaste of God's reign. The church lives as an alien and stranger in its own society because the Spirit forms it as God's new society.

Mystery

The Old Testament is the story of God's dealings with Israel, which exists only as a gift of God's mercy. In the desperate state of slavery, the Hebrew people cry out to God for deliverance. The texts tell us that the Lord hears their cries and remembers his covenant with Abraham. He determines to deliver this group of nobodies and pull them out of a slavery that would have resulted in their extermination from the face of the earth (Exod. 2:23–24). They would have become like so many other marginalized groups—simply erased from the face of the earth as of no importance or value in civilization.

The question must be asked: Why did God choose these people out of all the peoples of the earth? The only explanation is that *God* chose. The biblical narrative of slavery and deliverance invites us to recognize that this is a story in which the meaning of the events and the reasons for the thriving of this people cannot be explained simply in terms of historical events. It is not sufficient to say there was a great man named Moses who led an uprising. The texts will not permit this rationale. Neither can these events be explained by a plea to the human longing for freedom that motivated these people to break loose of their chains like some ancient precursors of myths about the founding of America.

Israel's existence just can't be explained in terms of human action or preference. Israel does not exist because Abram chose to leave Ur of the Chaldees or Moses turned aside to see a burning bush. It was not because of the genius of leaders or great individuals that Israel came into being when her people were about to disappear from the face of the earth. The biblical narratives simply announce that God chose these people, and that is the only explanation for Israel's existence. There is no moral balance sheet that tipped things in favor of this people over all others. The biblical story is not about these people but about God and the mystery of his choosing. This choosing is like nothing else in the world, but it makes the world what it is.

The New Testament is shaped by a similar mystery of God's choosing. Why were *these* people and not others chosen to form the church? The texts relate a sense of awe about this choosing. It is a mystery, but not the kind we normally think of when we call things a mystery today. Commonly a mystery is something for which we

41

as yet don't have enough information to explain, as in the sentence: "Her medical condition is a mystery." The assumption here is that at some point in the future there will be enough information to provide a perfectly reasonable, rational explanation. On the contrary, the biblical texts tell us that there aren't such explanations to make sense of what is happening in the story. The mystery is that God has chosen to act, and we cannot and will not find any explanation beyond his choosing and acting. This is a radically different understanding of mystery from our usual assumptions and interpretations.

The mysterious choosing of the people of Israel forms the imaginative backdrop to the New Testament concept of *election*. The mystery of the election of the church is not, as in Augustine's framing, about who has been selected by God to escape judgment and get in the lifeboat to heaven called *church*. It is not about which individuals were chosen and which were left out. Like the choosing of Israel in Abram, this choosing is not really about those inside the church but about *being chosen by God to represent him for the sake of the world.*

The deepest mystery is the existence of the church. Here in this strange, mixed, social community known as the *ecclesia* of God is where he has chosen to make present the mystery of creation. It is also where the empowering work of Christ and the Spirit are present and expressed in the world (Eph. 1:15–23). The question can be asked as to why God chose to act in this way. Why did God call the church into being? Why did God choose the kinds of people who were chosen—people Paul describes as the "offscouring" of the earth (1 Cor. 4:13 NKJV)—among whom resides nothing that would make them our choice for the transformation of creation? No matter how many times we ask these kinds of questions, there is an irreducible mystery, a surpassing wonder. Those called into the church did not choose to join a voluntary society; they are called and chosen by God. They are called to be a sign, witness, and foretaste of God's coming kingdom. To participate in the missional journey is to embrace this mystery and allow this reality to overwhelm and supersede the pressing matters of being a successful church or growing the church, which seem to dominate our imaginations.

Memory

Memory sustains the people of Israel in the Old Testament and forms them into a people with a peculiar identity. The same is the case of the church in the New Testament. What is meant by the term *memory* since, as we will see below, it is used differently in Scripture than we use it today? In Scripture, memory is what the skeleton is to the body—without it, all collapses into an insubstantial mess. Israel knew that it only existed because of its attention to its memory (Deut. 6:20–25). Memory and the rehearsal of that memory forms Israel—not just any kind of memory, but a very specific memory rooted in events and stories of God's actions to, for, and with Israel. The Old Testament recounts how these people continually worked with their memory of the founding stories of God's actions with them. Israel understood that once this memory was lost, so also was its distinctiveness as a people. This is why so much emphasis was placed on the ongoing rehearsal of its memory.

Modern cultures have lost touch with the form of memory understood in the biblical narratives. For us the idea of memory is akin to quaint recollections about the past captured in scrapbooks or home videos that represent what has been but is no longer. Memory for us is about what is in the past but has no living power in the present or nostalgia for an earlier period that has gone.

The biblical narratives present a radically different understanding of memory. The memory of God's choosing and acting is never confined to the past; it lives in the present and shapes the future. It is the reliving and reenacting of past events in the present because these events continue to have power and are the primary shapers of life.

The Feast of the Passover is an example. It relives and celebrates the first Passover, and in so doing it continually re-forms the people of God, giving them their present identity. This is why the language of remembering and forgetting is so prevalent in the Old Testament; to forget is to cease to be who you are as a people. In this sense the opposite of remembering is not forgetting so much as dismembering. The language of memory in the Old Testament is formed with powerful images and metaphors, such as: "If I forget you, O Jerusalem, may my right hand forget its skill. May my tongue cling to the roof of my mouth" (Ps. 137:5–6). In the book of Jeremiah the words of the prophet about the judgment of God toward Jerusalem aren't primarily about moral failure, they are cast in terms of forgetting, of losing the memory of what has been done and of who they are as God's people. This recognizes that remembering is about being shaped and formed by a way of life in the present that determines the future. In this sense there can be no appropriate future without memory.

The same understanding is operative in the New Testament. The church exists as a church so long as it lives in the story about the life, death, and resurrection of Jesus Christ and the outpouring of the Holy Spirit. Outside of this memory the church cannot exist as God intends. But this understanding of its life is only available through the present, lived remembering of the story. This is why at the center of Christian worship is the Eucharist. The lived memory determines the church's life and practice. The way the Eucharist is practiced makes clear the depth of the church's captivity to modernity. Denominations birthed in modernity limit the Lord's Supper to a memorial—a modern remembering of a past event. This truncated, reductionistic expression of the meal reveals how far we are from the understanding of memory present in Scripture.

What does this memory do? In contradistinction to modernity, memory forms us into the people of God who live by an alternative story whose power shapes the present. As such, this community formed in the mystery of God's choosing is being shaped as a parallel culture because it is grasped by a present, lived memory of the story. This is the strange new world of the Bible that is absent from the memory of men and women in North America. For most people attending a Protestant service, for example, the Lord's Table is little more than a chance to have a personal, private moment of remembering and feeling (emotion) before moving back into a world disconnected from this moment of feeling. The result is that, for example, there is little engagement with the Lord's Table as a place where we are formed into practices that shape the whole of our life as a people. Missional church is about a people of memory being continually formed in practices that shape us as an alternative story in our culture.

44

Mission

Mission is the outgrowth of mystery and memory. Israel is called for the sake of the world. Abram is called from Ur of the Chaldees (Genesis 12) to form a people through whom all the earth will be blessed. Mission is not an action or program but the essence that pervades all the church is. God calls the church to be the demonstration of what all creation is to be. Likewise, the church is the new Israel (Luke 12:32; 1 Pet. 2:9–10), called for the sake of the world. Mission is not something the church does as an activity; it is what the church *is* through the mystery of its formation and memory of its calling. The church is God's missionary people. There is no participation in Christ without participation in God's mission in the world. The church in North America to a large extent has lost this memory to the point that mission is but a single element in multifaceted, programmatic congregations serving the needs of the members. The gospel is now a religious message that meets the needs of self-actualizing individuals. But the North American church is being invited by the boundary-breaking Spirit to discover once again its nature as God's missionary people. This will mean going against the stream of most church life at this moment in time.[4]

Earlier in this chapter, we saw why *missional church* cannot be codified in a simple definition. It is more than a new word for *evangelism*, church planting, or meeting someone in a coffee shop for conversation. It is not about restructuring or a new program. Missional church is about an alternative imagination for being the church. It is about this transformation toward a church that is shaped by *mystery*, *memory*, and *mission*.

3

Does *Missional* Fit?

Can My Church Be Missional?

If we don't have a clear definition and can't point to a model, can we at least see what kinds of churches are doing this missional thing? In other words, how do I know if *missional* fits my church? Lutherans want to know if this is for the mainline, Baptists want to be missional among their own churches, and so on. There are an endless number of church types in North America, and if we think in terms of programs or models, usually certain types of churches line up with certain types of programs. But if being missional is not about a program or model, then how do we know if it fits?

There is no simple answer to these questions. Across multiple church systems the missional conversation has taken on a life of its own. Books, conferences, and websites offer a variety of proposals and models for missional life that are taken up by denominations and churches of every stripe. As a result people access resources and ideas from one another, often crossing traditional lines of denominations or affiliations. This kind of boundary crossing means that the missional conversation, in all its current forms, can enter practically any kind of church right now. This raises questions about how the missional conversation relates to the various categories of church, such as:

- How does missional church relate to emergent church?
- Can a megachurch become a missional church?
- Can a traditional church with a building become missional?
- Are so-called *organic* churches missional?
- Is a missional church a house church or small group gathering?
- Can a rural, mainline church become missional?
- Is this an urban reality, or can a suburban church become missional?

We could respond with a *yes* or *no* to each question, but it's not that simple. The missional conversation transcends these categories. Lutherans, Emergents, Mennonites, Presbyterians, and others are asking similar questions about the church. Traditional church, emergent church, house church, and megachurch leaders are wrestling with questions about being the church today. In the radically different contexts of suburban, urban, and rural congregations, the questions are the same.

A comment by a seminary president drives home the point: "I have just been made president of a seminary that trains leaders for a world that doesn't exist anymore. A few years ago I would never have come to a meeting like this with leaders from such radically different traditions and outlooks about the church. But we are all in the same boat now. We all know that business as usual won't address the challenges we face, and we know that our traditions have run out of gas in terms of helping us communicate with this new world. We are all here because the missional conversation is one that doesn't divide us and the one that is asking the right questions."

Honest church leaders realize that we are all in a period of massive transition that is leading us down a new path. We are all novices searching for a way of being the church. The challenge we face is that our questions about missional church are primarily about how to fix what we have already been doing. We know how to do attractional church: multisite models are simply new ways of being attractional, small group structures are usually formed to organize those attracted to the weekend services, and evangelism systems are designed to get people to come to church. But a missional imagination can't be squeezed into such models.

How the Missional Church Transcends Categorization

There are many different denominations, parachurch agencies, and church networks in North America as well as newer movements and networks that transcend traditional denominational boundaries. We are in a period of a major reshaping of church life. Some established denominations are declining or going through huge transitions while new networks and associations are being born. The figures vary depending on who is reporting on the research,[1] but all agree that fewer and fewer people are shaped by earlier denominational loyalties, and a growing percentage of Christians are dropping out of existing churches altogether. We are in a period of flux and experimentation, and no one knows where it is all going. Suburban congregations aren't growing as they once did. Many urban churches and those in the first rings of suburbanization struggle to survive. Seeker churches, the model in the 1980s and 1990s, are questioning the reasons that brought them success. But we are also witnessing the rapid development of house, organic, and emergent churches.

Does missional fit these various traditions, networks, and affiliations? *Yes!* At the same time, if one wants to lay the missional over or add it to our known ways of being the church, we would answer with an equally bold *No!* This missional journey calls us out onto a new kind of river that none of us know how to navigate, because it challenges the core of our church imaginations.

Missional is a way of being the church that can be expressed in many different forms, traditions, structures, and sizes. Over the past five years the missional conversation has entered a broad set of streams and dialogues about the church. Here are some examples of people and groups who have taken on the missional language as part of their identity:

Emergent Churches

- Karen Ward, abbess of the Church of the Apostle in Seattle, Washington, is part of a monastic, incarnational Christian community running a neighborhood coffee shop in her beloved neighborhood.
- Kevin Rains is part of a Christian community in Cincinnati, Ohio, that consists of two communal homes where people agree to live by strict missional orders as they seek to live faithfully in their city.
- Rudy Carrasco lives in Pasadena, California, and is part of an urban ministry to children, youth, and families—bridging the Hispanic and African-American communities in his neighborhood.
- Ben Edson in Sanctus 1, Manchester, England, draws young urbanites into fresh expressions of church focused around the creative arts.
- Jonny Baker, part of Church Army in the United Kingdom, runs creative experiments in missional life.

Traditional Churches

- Steve Taylor joined a ninety-six-year-old fractured and dying Baptist church in Christchurch, New Zealand. It is now comprised of many people on mission in their community.
- Chris Erdman, senior pastor of University Presbyterian Church in Fresno, California, is leading a traditional pulpit church into new mission in its neighborhood. He has also developed a way of preaching that highlights what is going on through the church and moves people into mission.[2]

Rural Congregations

- Bill Rose-Heim is executive minister with the Disciples of Christ in rural Missouri. He established a network of part-time staff who cultivate missional life. Out of Bill's work has come a robust imagination for missional life in rural communities.
- Dave Dawson is executive presbyter of the Shanango Presbytery in northwestern Pennsylvania. The presbytery is comprised

of historic small town and rural churches. A well-informed, widely read missiologist, Dave has led the presbytery through a missional innovation in which people and churches are finding fresh ways to express kingdom life in their communities.

Megachurches

- In Glendale, Arizona, the Community of Joy under the leadership of Walt Kallestad has been moving through a process of missional transformation. Walt invited a team from the United Kingdom to join the church several years ago and journey with them in the formation of missional life. This is a huge undertaking as a purely attractional, seeker-based church begins the turn toward intentional missional life.
- Scott (coauthor of this book) is one of the pastors at a large church in Saint Paul, Minnesota. For years it has attracted many people through its doors and cast a radical vision for the kingdom. Many have caught that vision and ventured out and started creative ministries in their neighborhoods, often starting their own ministries. Then it occurred to the leadership that this should be the focus of the future of the church rather than an anomaly only pursued by radical entrepreneur types. Now the leaders have restructured the church to invite people, many of whom attend for consumeristic reasons, on a journey of reframing so they can form a network of missional communities that will be spread throughout the Twin Cities.

Denominations

- Several years ago Mennonites across North America merged into a new denomination called the Mennonite Church USA. The merger was approved because it would self-identify as a missional denomination.
- In the past several years the Disciples of Christ have been shaping a series of national transformation meetings, at the center of which is the question of how to form missional conferences.
- Under the leadership of Paul Cameron, the Churches of Christ in Melbourne, Australia, is five years into a process that is wit-

nessing a movement in local churches to discover missional life.

- In the United Kingdom the Church of England and the Methodist denomination have teamed together to develop Fresh Expressions as a mission-shaped initiative that is seeing thousands of ordinary men and women in local churches move into their communities and networks with missional initiatives.

The missional conversation has entered almost every stream of the church. The Spirit of God is moving in the church in creative, generative ways that call the people of God to engage their neighborhoods and display God's kingdom in everyday life. In fact, church leaders are confessing that they know how to build church programs and promote church activities but have missed out on participating in God's kingdom life. Even within some of the most prominent attractional churches, there are missional experiments. Large churches are empowering people to listen to what God is doing outside the church buildings and blessing them to follow God's leading without having to call it a ministry of that church.

Mark Priddy had made his home in Eagle, Idaho, since moving his business there from Southern California. His family had settled into a large church in downtown Boise where the children attended a private school. Everyone's life had grown increasingly busy with the rounds of church meetings and driving kids to all kinds of events. Without a clear sense of direction but a growing dissatisfaction with the craziness of life, Mark and Jeanette pulled the kids out of private school, considered how to form church in their neighborhood, and gathered some friends to pray with them. They soon became aware of the kids in the community and the fact that there were few places for them to connect.

At that time a building was put up for auction by the fire department. It seemed to offer all the group was looking for as a potential place for kids to gather. Priddy dropped by the room where the auction was being held about ten minutes before bidding closed. When he asked what the current bid was, he was told there were no bids in. Priddy wrote a ridiculously low number on a piece of paper, and the Lord provided them with the building.

From these initial gatherings for prayer and the desire to follow God into the neighborhood, an amazing set of relationships developed, out of which came the Landing.[3] After the youth center came into being, so did a counseling center, a home for the local ballet group, and initiatives to engage poverty and serve the elderly in the community. All of this emerged from a small gathering of Christians who knew God was calling them back into their neighborhood to enter people's stories and discover what the Spirit wanted to do among people. Having received the Idaho Brightest Star Award in 2005 as well as the 2006 Humanitarian Award from the city, today the Landing is a center of life in Eagle and an outstanding example of the conviction that God is up to something in the local contexts in which we live.

A new imagination is being formed within these people. They realize that simply calling something missional is not the point. They know that it is much more than church planting or some form of a house church. They have opened themselves up and ventured out on an experimental journey into their neighborhoods to see what God is up to in this world.

What Is the Difference between a Missional and an Emergent Imagination?

Some people assume churches that self-identify as emergent are by definition missional. But the *emergent* label is attached to many different kinds of churches. Some are producing rich, creative experiments; many seek to recover the riches of spiritual disciplines and liturgy within the Christian tradition. Emergent churches embrace what they call the *postmodern turn* in seeking an understanding of reason that is more than a set of rationalistic propositions. Through the arts and the encouragement of creativity they provide wonderful opportunities to engage with Scripture and younger adults. These churches tend to be gatherings shaped by the desire for celebration and the formation of community that is local and networked. Some even emphasize the local community as the place where church is formed and deliberately resist becoming churches where people drive distances to buildings for meetings but rarely have extended relationships outside formal meeting times. They experiment with new forms of worship and spirituality that emphasize ancient practices and more aesthetic, earthbound forms of worship. All of this is a wonderful gift to the body of Christ.

The emergent and missional streams, however, are not necessarily the same thing. Many emergent churches seem to be new forms of attractional churches that have little sense of their neighborhoods or the missional nature of the church. The church has long sought to do church services and events in relevant ways to attract different segments of society—the seeker service being the most prominent in its aim to reach middle-class Baby Boomers. Some emergent churches are leading in the missional conversation, charting new paths for the rest of us. But the category of emergent and the imagination of missional are two different things.

The Sending of the Church

The subtitle of the book *The Missional Church* is *A Vision for the Sending of the Church in North America*, which was intended to say that the church is more than an organization providing spiritual goods and services in order to be successful. It is a recognition that the church is missional in nature. At its core is the reality that God's people are a sign to the world of who God is. This missional nature cannot be subdivided into internal activities for insiders and external activities for outsiders. All the church does and is should live out God's life in the midst of the world; missional people should practice God's life before a watching world. This includes worship, preaching, communion, loving one another, social justice, caring for the poor, and sharing Jesus's gospel. Being missional is about all of it, not part. This is the missional imagination. All of God's people are on mission to engage their surrounding neighborhoods, not just a few who are sent outside the church to do something called missions. Figure 7 illustrates this.

While this diagram is necessarily simplistic, it introduces the imagination of being missional fleshed out in more depth in the rest of the book. Notice that this illustration emphasizes the call of God to be his people in the midst of life, engaging everyday life in the

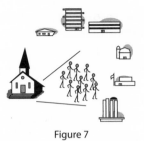

Figure 7

neighborhoods where they live. It is not about making the church structures and programs and all the machinations work better. It is about the sending of God's peculiar people into the midst of the world to engage people in their neighborhoods and demonstrate together God's life.

Questions about whether missional *fits my church* are often based on the hope of becoming a better attractional or attractional-missionary church. This is not surprising. The attractional imagination is our default. It has shaped us to believe we can just preach God's vision and people will get on board. It has convinced us that if we build the right program with the best training and curriculum, "they will come." It has formed us to believe that all we need to do is meet a felt need and then people will respond. People are asking questions about this attractional form of church, but they struggle to understand the problem it represents.

A lay leader who had been the CEO of a large grocery chain described the energetic new pastor who had come to his church several years earlier. This pastor was a good preacher who had many creative ideas for innovative programs in the church. The retired CEO was very astute. Although he was committed to the church and pastor, he recognized the problem: "But all we are doing is growing on the backs of other churches. We're attracting people from other churches and celebrating our growth. We haven't had an adult baptism in years!" The CEO intuitively knew that the pastor's plan might meet the current expectations of church life, but he was looking for something else that would fit them better.

When we don't see this attractional focus for what it is, we keep trying to fit being missional into it. As a result the attractional shuts down the transformational capacity of the missional. Loading missional onto the already burdened lives of men and women in our congregations will not form missional life. A new imagination can't be added on top of an old one. Therefore it is helpful to understand what hinders our ability to embrace this new missional imagination.

Dams That Block the Flow of Missional Life

Canada's national animal is the beaver. This amazing water creature is seen across the country in lake areas. The beavers' claim to fame is the dams they build in rivers and shallow lakes. These dams stop water from flowing into the surrounding rivers and streams, potentially interfering with other wildlife in the river and occasionally creating significant problems for commerce in that area. Sometimes the dams have to be removed to return the river to its vital flow of life.

We have worked with churches that have been *beaver-dammed*—their way of being church blocks the flow of God's mystery, memory, and mission. Such churches think they can become missional by adding programs of outreach, but they miss the internal dynamics blocking their ability to enter into a different imagination about themselves and what God might be up to in their neighborhoods. These churches think they are becoming missional when they merely are circling around a lake that has resulted from the dammed river.

In the previous chapter we said a missional life is engaged as we enter the narratives of the Scriptures at the levels of mystery, memory, and mission. To do this we need to recognize what has become dammed up in our churches and, consequently, the kinds of waters in which we are currently navigating. We do see, for example, that in our own culture the church has been largely turned into a provider of spiritual goods and services for self-actualizing individuals. This is not a missional river but a dammed, stagnant pool that can give no life to the kingdom Jesus announced. This stagnant pool represents the way of doing church that has resulted in a private, spiritual enclave that is actually closed off from the fast, running waters of missional life.

Table 2 shows some of the ways the missional waters of mystery, memory, and mission have been dammed up and hindered from flowing. It looks at two specific dams shaping the churches today—the modern and the postmodern.

Table 2

Modernity Is about Erasing Origins	Postmodernity Is about Borrowing Origins
Reduces *mystery* to history, chance, or preference.	Reduces *mystery* to spiritual options and experiences.
Replaces *memory* with: Progress Future Next Frontier	Replaces *memory* with nostalgia, borrowing bits and pieces from every kind of tradition to assemble its own brief experience in the present moment.
Recasts mission as self-actualization.	Recasts *mission* with playfulness because it has no need to indwell any story or be shaped by anything external to the present. It emphasizes in-the-moment experience of the self or the affinity group.

Modernity   I could flesh out this concept in class

The first dam is called *modernity*—a term used to describe the worldview that took shape in the West over the past several centuries. Our purpose here is not to give a broad description of modernity or explain the philosophy behind it. We simply aim to identify some places where it has created blockages to missional life.

What follows should not be viewed as modernity bashing; many of its forms of thought, creativity, and technology have transformed the world for the better. Both of us are using Apple laptop computers to write this book, and we often communicate with one another with our iPhones. When Alan was in the Toronto airport on his way to England, he was working on this chapter and was also constantly in touch with his wife, who had just had dental surgery in Vancouver. All of this is a gift of modernity. We are not exponents of the idea that modernity is over, thrown up on the garbage heap of history as we move into the brave new world of the postmodern. Instead, in this section we seek to peel back some of the core assumptions of modernity to help us see the challenges we face in forming missional life.

That being said, elements of modernity lead to the elimination of *mystery* from its vocabulary because it deems the word to represent a kind of obscurantism that is afraid of using the mind to solve tough problems. In this sense, modernity tends to turn everything in the world into objective, observable facts that can be accounted for and adequately described with either historical or scientific categories. This is what people like Richard Dawkins and Christopher Hitchens do in their respective books *The God Delusion* and *God Is Not Great*.[4] They each trade on the assumption of modernity that all mystery is but an excuse for flabby thinking and superstition.

One of the marks of modernity is its quest for measurable, countable certainty, which has resulted in an attempt to make everything explainable and controllable. This is exhibited in the dominance of the historical-critical method of biblical studies in the last century. Anyone who went to seminary was trained in this method as a way of explaining and codifying a text by breaking it into parts to understand the way it was put together. We are not saying the method is wrong but that it became the primary method of interpreting Scripture. As a result the biblical narrative was displaced and reinterpreted through these categories of modern research. Mystery was removed; the Bible became explainable to modern people as a story understood within the limits of reason alone. It became a managed text that ceased to have meaning as the unexplainable story of a peculiar God who chooses a people and acts through them for the sake of the world.

This loss of mystery is represented in the way churches use demographic information. It is amazing that churches pay thousands of dollars to buy well-packaged data that is supposed to tell them who lives in the surrounding areas of their church and what their interests and needs are. It's not that demographic information is unhelpful; rather, the problem is that we believe that through abstract, scientific information we can actually remove the mystery and know the people in our communities. It is also a terrible confession to our loss of ability to simply sit with other human beings in the mystery of who they are and get to know them through ordinary, simple conversation.

Modernity also tends to replace *memory* with its obverse: the continual creation of the new and the next. The North American myths of the new land, the new frontier, and new ideas are images of modernity's most compelling and destructive attachment to progress.

In this sense the past should be dismissed, moved past, reduced to history, and displaced by the ever-rolling tide of an inevitable, bold new future. So deep is this conviction within us that we believe it is possible to start all over again with a clean slate. This imagination shapes the way church leaders plan and measure success. For moderns the past is not the source that shapes the present; it is not a living memory that forms a people. Rather, the past is an obstacle that keeps getting in the way of the new and the next. As a result the great traditions of the church are set aside for the new and the next church method that arises. Church leadership is reduced to an endless search for a method to find success. When we read the Bible in this kind of environment, we read it as a personal help manual, as a guidebook for living life well in a self-actualization culture, or as guidance for finding a God who will meet my needs when the future doesn't go according to plan or the goods and services purchased at the mall don't satisfy in quite the right way. God then becomes a way to improve my life.

Modernity replaces *mission* with self-actualization of the expressive, autonomous individual. When we attend to the way people talk about the gospel, it does not take long to discover just how much the focus lies on meeting personal needs. During testimony sessions about mission trips, people explain how it changed them or how it gave them an experience they will never forget. In modernity the purpose of life is to fulfill one's personal destiny, goals, or needs. When modern people encounter the biblical story, what they read is a text that invites them into personal wholeness, self-discovery with God, and individual development in a spiritual life. In fact, modernity has shaped our understanding of the gospel, mission, and the biblical story so that many if not most respond to this critique with: "Isn't this what the gospel is about?" For moderns, it's almost impossible to read the biblical narrative without assimilating it to the modern categories of the self and the fulfillment of its needs.

In Scripture, mission calls a people into a radically different vision on a journey bigger and other than ourselves. Scripture calls us into the memory of an amazing story of celebrative life—not for ourselves but for the sake of the world. The strangeness of this story is its illogical nature and irrepressible meaning: find life by losing it; only by leaving the places of security are the purposes of

God discovered. The God revealed in Scripture gives himself away for the sake of the world.

Postmodernity

The second dam that shapes the church today is *postmodernity*. This is an interesting term to describe, because the idea of calling something *post* is to say we know where we have been but not where we are now. As stated above, we are not convinced we have suddenly entered the end of modernity, but we do know that modernity is taking some new turns and many are calling these *postmodern*. Some of these so-called postmodern turns are certainly reactions to some of modernity's own overstretching and overclaiming. Take, for example, the questions of *mystery*. In the new space where we find ourselves, there has been a reaction to modernity's reading of mystery, but it has not been a return to the way the biblical narratives use the term. The postmodern seems to reduce mystery to spiritual options as a reaction to the cold objectification of all reality and its absolute categorizing within the limits of reason (modern rationality) alone.

The recent writings of Tolle Eckhardt are an example of this move. For instance, *A New Earth* promises to enlighten the reader to the secret to inner harmony and awareness of purpose. His books are massive bestsellers as people hunger for some connections with the world that aren't objectified or result-driven. In this sense, the so-called postmodern seems to turn the notion of mystery into the discovery of some inner spirituality connected with a reenchantment of the world—the primacy of nonrational and noncognitive experiences. It is not so much about the mystery of God's choosing as the possibility of expressing personal preferences in embracing, for brief periods of time, multiple options of spiritual experiences for one's own personal taste and experimentation. It's more like Oprah than Jesus. In this sense of the postmodern, biblical mystery is again subsumed beneath the categories of personal taste, ego experimentation, and an openness to all or anything that may be encountered in an ephemeral spiritual realm of life.

The postmodern turn reconnects with *memory* in all sorts of ways. This reconnecting, however, is not shaped by the memory of a story but creates nostalgic experiences in the moment. Nostalgia and experiences of the moment are different from memory.[5] The biblical narrative tells us that only by living inside and being shaped by a definitive story, by never forgetting that story, and by reliving it as memory in ritual and repetition is it possible to be formed into a people who live by an alternative story. This is why the weekly Eucharist practiced with other Christians is so important. Memory forms a people.

Nostalgia, however, is not about being formed as a people; it is about borrowing experiences and moments from the past in order to experience something for ourselves in the present. Nostalgic individuals link themselves to a historically specific time or event in order to serve their personal desires for an experience in the moment. It is all about resourcing the self by consuming the past. It produces a simulation of the past—like the middle-aged man who purchases a Harley-Davidson in order to live in the myth of the youthful, unfettered individual who is free to go anywhere at any time. The church in North America lives too much by borrowing and creating nostalgic moments; too much of our worship events are media-driven uses of nostalgia to create moments of personal experience in a crowd of strangers. Too little does it live into the memory of its story; it is largely forgotten by most who come to church buildings looking for moments of spiritual engagement to resource the thinness of their disembedded, fragmented lives. The missional imagination calls us to discern the differences between nostalgia and memory.

Postmodernity takes the idea of *mission* as the central meaning of life and turns it into playfulness in the moment. If Abram leaving Ur of the Chaldees and Jesus hanging on a cross are signs of God's movement for the sake of the world, the postmodern signs are seen in television programs like *Friends* or *Sex in the City*. The mission of a person's life is reduced and located in the small, self-enclosed world of affinity groups—the core, safe group of people who truly belong to one another. Instead of mission for the sake of God's creation, it is reduced to protecting our kind or sealing off our group from others. We wish we could say that the church is immune to this mind-set, but much of the focus in the church has become about church survival or turning around churches for the sake of preserving the church as it is known.

Modernity and postmodernity are two dams that hinder the flow of mission in most churches. Just because the dams exist in no way precludes a church from entering the missional river. *Missional* fits all kinds of churches in all kinds of places and traditions, but it only fits when we enter into the biblical view of mystery, memory, and mission and discern the contours of the missional imagination. We begin to understand that it is far more than retrofitting all the attractional programs and evangelism strategies we now have by calling them missional. In order to travel the missional river, we all have dams we must tear down first. And we have both discovered that we have to revisit old dams that we thought were gone and relearn what God's view of mystery, memory, and mission really is. This is not something we simply overcome and then move on. We are learning to see the world differently. We are learning to see God and the church differently. The Spirit of God is moving in our midst to reshape us and clear the river for the missional church in our day.

Part 2

THREE MISSIONAL CONVERSATIONS

4

What's Behind the Wardrobe?

The Center of the Missional Church

Alan sat with the volunteer leaders of several churches as they described some of the missional experiments in their local churches. These leaders weren't describing new programs or a model of a healthy church that they had used; instead they were telling stories of engaging people in their neighborhoods. They talked about listening to the ways God was already at work in their communities. They shared about inviting neighbors over for meals and talking together about life with new friends around them. They had discovered that *missional* wasn't about a new program or project inside a church but about entering their community to sit alongside others and engage in gospel conversations. It was changing the ways they were being the church.

In C. S. Lewis's *The Lion, the Witch and the Wardrobe*, there's an old wardrobe in the attic that leads to another world. To go beyond the wardrobe is to enter a world shaped by a radically different imagination about how things work. Over the last several years, growing numbers of Christians have sought to discover the path into a missional life. A pastor in the Midwest began to spend some time outside the doors and demands of her congregation to connect with people where she lived. Initially she walked her dog through the community in the late afternoon as people were coming home from work. In the midst of those walks she began bumping into people from a few streets over who belonged to a housing development. They struck up conversations, and before she knew it they were talking to each other about the neighborhood and what was happening in the community. Previously the pastor had no idea about the people who lived in her neighborhood, but now she was wrestling with fresh questions about new friends who were not going to cross the barriers to come to her church. What was she to do with these new friends? What did it mean to form and be the church in her neighborhood? How might she share these stories with her friends in the church, and what did it mean for ministry? She was being stretched, and her imagination of what church was about was being challenged.

In a suburb of Edmonton a medical doctor and his family had been heavily invested in a growing attractional church for many years. Then a family crisis caused him to recognize that he had not spent the time with his late teen and early twenties children as he had wanted. Over the period of several years he took each of them individually on trips overseas where they lived and served among people in difficult life situations for extended periods of time. In the midst of these journeys he realized that in all his busyness he had not stopped to connect with the people in his own neighborhood. He decided to do a small thing to change that by crossing the street each week to mow the lawn of a shut-in neighbor. He had no plans bigger than just wanting to connect and serve his neighborhood. After some months he was cutting not one but four lawns on the street. Instead of each one taking only about ten minutes, each was taking him thirty to forty minutes because neighbors were coming out to talk with him. Before long he and his wife were inviting people over for coffee and then for barbeques and community events. None of this was a plan; it simply tumbled out as he connected with and cared for his neighborhood. As this happened, his imagination about Christian life and church was challenged. He wondered why he was commuting twenty minutes to go to church and attend all the meetings when he felt they were distracting him from what he sensed God was doing in his own neighborhood. Without even a conscious decision, he found himself leading Bible studies in the neighborhood, and what seemed to be emerging was a neighborhood church among people who wouldn't get in a car and drive to church. He found himself taken along in a stream of surprise and unexpected new life.

Risk takers find themselves going through the wardrobe and tumbling into a new imagination about being God's people. From the other side of the wardrobe it seems to them that the attractional churches are stuck in an old attic where they can't see what the Spirit is doing in neighborhoods and communities. This kind of people wants to invite others to venture with them into the world beyond the wardrobe, but they are unsure how to do it because it feels like disloyalty to their current churches. How does one communicate the mystery of the ways God is moving in mission when so many have lost the memory of what the church is meant to be?

On the other hand, there are others working hard managing life in the attic while talking about the world on the other side of the wardrobe. They are honestly struggling to find ways of inviting their churches to take a risk in a new world and finding it hard to convince them. Still others have decided the church in the attic isn't worth the effort—the sooner it dies the better.

Our reading of Scripture keeps telling us that God's future almost always breaks out among those in real-life attic situations, moving through imperfect people and structures. God is always going to surprise us by calling forth a new imagination in all the places we want to write off.

Whether they are on the other side of the wardrobe or sitting in the attic, all churches in the West are being forced to ask questions about what it means to be God's people today. We find ourselves in the midst of turbulent change that is disrupting our widely accepted patterns of church life. In a meeting of Mennonite leaders where such questions were being addressed, one man in his sixties said, "Listen, our children are losing their jobs—we are in a new place of crisis." His point was in what he didn't say, namely, everyone was feeling that the difficult changes in their world were compelling them to ask hard questions about the kind of church God was calling forth from them. There are huge changes under way in our world that are pressing hard against our assumed practices of church and causing us to reimagine what it means to be God's people.

Conversations about the Missional Church

We are all seeking to become people who enter the river that is formed by mystery, memory, and mission, but we need practical ways to invite people into conversations about what it means to enter this river. We have found that there are three basic topics to help people understand what it means to be missional. As people converse about these three topics, they find themselves moving toward the river and seeing practical ways to engage the questions we face during these turbulent times.

1. Reconsidering Our Context—the West Is Now a Mission Field

In 2002 a major British tabloid published a front-page interview with a Catholic bishop under the headline: "Christianity Has Almost Expired in the UK!" This may be a hyperbole, but it is a telling confession. The same comment could be made for most of Western Europe. Similarly, in Canada a majority of the emerging generations have no memory of the Christian narrative. Twenty years ago this was not the case. The shift has been dramatic and swift. Corrosive forces of change had been building for decades under the surface of popular culture, and then suddenly they reached the tipping point as the culture shifted like a great earthquake. America is not far behind. It's already happening in various regions. Beneath the façade of suburban megachurches are growing numbers of people (Christians) who want nothing to do with the church as it is.

We face a radically new challenge in the West that requires more than minor adjustments or course corrections. We need a new imagination for being the church. We need local churches to become mission agencies in their neighborhoods and communities. This is more than tweaking programs or doing demographic surveys. For some of us it is difficult to see how to do this.

Scott understood all this in theory, but he grew up in a Southern Baptist church in the Bible Belt that made it very hard for him to see how it was possible to form a different kind of church. Because he understood how "missions" worked, he began to ask the questions of a foreign missionary:

68

- If I were part of a team who moved to Asia to share the gospel with people who naturally reject Jesus, how would we shape our lives?
- What would we take with us and what would we discard?
- What would be our stance? Would we come with ready-made answers or dialogue and listen?

Scott saw he had to let go of much of what he knew about church and how to communicate the gospel. He then was able to ask different questions of his local church:

- What is the gospel when people expect Jesus to meet their private spiritual needs but nothing else?
- How can we reach people in our neighborhoods who just aren't going to come to church?
- How do I find out what God is already up to in the neighborhood?
- What kind of church might the Spirit want to shape in this neighborhood?

He found himself asking neighborhood, rather than church, questions and focusing on how the gospel relates to a local situation, not how the church could be more attractional.

2. Rethinking the Gospel—the Missio Dei

Usually when we think about the church and effective church strategies, the focus lies on what works. Rarely are the practical questions about church connected to theology. Conversation about the missional church should be informed by a Latin phrase that is deeply rooted in theology: *missio dei* ("mission of God"). One of the ways the basic story of the gospel has been compromised is that it has become all about us and how God is supposed to meet our needs, and we have created attractional churches that are about how God does just that. This deforms God's story. It makes us—Western, middle-class people who are the richest, most blessed human beings who have ever lived—the subject and object of the gospel. This is not liberating good news; it is a terrible, malformed captivity to ourselves. The gospel story is about God, not us; it is about what God is doing for the sake of the world, not about meeting the needs of self-actualizing, middle-class, Western people. The phrase *missio dei* attempts to say this in what may seem a strange way, but its intent is to say to the church: "Wake up!" We have been traveling down a terribly dead-end, fetid, stinking river that is all about us and our own reflections. *Missio dei* calls us to see that God is up to something radically different than we imagined and that there is another vibrant, powerful, awesome river streaming toward us.

This all may seem obvious, but it's not. We are not focused on God's mission but on *how* God serves and meets our needs. Jesus is a packaged choice in the spiritual food court. We have a debased, compromised, sterilized Christianity. The biblical narratives revolve around God's mission in, through, and for the sake of the world. The focus is toward God. The *missio dei* is the understanding of Jesus's life, death, and resurrection that is centered on God rather than on meeting personal needs. Craig Van Gelder uses two questions to help people grapple with this: (1) What is God doing in this world? This calls for discernment to recognize what God is doing in our neighborhoods, schools, businesses, and so forth. (2) What does God want to do in our world? Each direct our attention and energy in a very different direction.

We are shaped by a version of the gospel that focuses on individuals. There is an unstated, pervasive assumption that God's salvation is for individuals, and if individuals will heed this message, they will have a better life. It can be a shattering experience to realize that while God came to save persons, God's grace does not revolve around me and my needs. It is God's story, and we are participants in his story and mission. This is why it's crucial to see the gospel in terms of mystery, memory, and mission.

3. Reimagining Church—Sign, Witness, and Foretaste of God's Dream for the World

Our culture continues to move through massive levels of change that are decentering the church. This change is forcing us to ask how we can be God's people in this pluralist culture where so much is up for grabs. One of the emerging responses from people like Lesslie

Newbigin is that the church is to be the sign and witness of God's dream for the world and to learn to do this in the neighborhoods and contexts of their people.

The Greek word used for church in the Bible was *ecclesia*. It wasn't a religious word but rather a political word meaning "a public assembly." Christians chose this word because they saw themselves and the church as a public *sign*, *witness*, and *foretaste* of where God was inviting all creation in Jesus Christ. A local church is to be an embodiment of what God is calling all creation to be through the Spirit. As a sign, witness, and foretaste, local churches should live as a contrast society right in the middle of their neighborhoods. It does this by inviting its people to transform their lives by developing habits such as those related in the stories told above: practicing hospitality, learning to be present in the community, and inviting those in their neighborhoods to taste and see what it means to be shaped by Jesus. Other important habits involve recovering some of the traditions of the church. (Further discussion of this is in chapter 7.) In movements such as New Monasticism and in focusing on recovering an emphasis on the local, we are witnessing the emergence of another stream of Christian energy that asks what some of the simple but profoundly transforming habits are that might shape us as sign, witness, and foretaste in our neighborhoods.

This is a stream that runs against the currents we have lived in to this point where the focus has been on our rights, our needs, our freedom to choose as we please, our freedom to cut and run whenever we get bored or it gets sticky and tough or things aren't quite working the way we expect. It is assumed that the appropriate means of living in a tolerant and open society is to create an environment that does not step on or over any specific set of personal rights, feelings, or desires. This is part of the madness of the *needs-centered*, *seeker-driven* mentality that has shaped so much of the church in North America. This new stream requires a shift of imagination into truly new waters.

A Three-Way Conversation

As mentioned in the introduction, Lesslie Newbigin returned to England after thirty years as a missionary to India, which allowed him to see his home country with the perspective of a concerned outsider. What he saw prompted him to ask fresh questions about Christian life in the West. Instead of asking abstract questions about what it means to be the church, he spoke of a three-way conversation between the gospel, the church, and the culture in which we live. He saw that being God's people in our time calls upon us to first ask about the interrelationship between the gospel and the context in which we live and then ask what it means to be the church. Our habit has been to ask these questions in the exact opposite way. First we ask about the nature and purpose of the church in some abstract or idealist way—for instance, we try to determine the *biblical* meaning of the church. Then we develop strategies to make this kind of church relevant to the places where we live. A missional understanding moves in a different direction, beginning with questions about the gospel and the context and then moving to the church so that the shape and life of the latter comes out of the interactions of the first two. One way to represent this conversation is with a triangle (see figure 8).

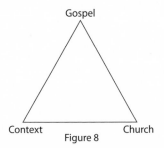

Figure 8

Being missional is not about *doing church* in a better way, nor is it about the *church* itself. There is much more. The leaders in a white church in a mid-American city decided that missional was the direction in which they needed to move. They managed to get the board to buy into this idea because the 1,500-member church was declining and losing most of its young people. The community around the church building had changed over the last decade and was now primarily Black-American. A decision was made to be missional to the Black community. A primary means to do this was to create an atrium where people could meet for coffee during the week. The idea was to attract the community into the church building and make it part of the community. At the same time, however, people inside the church were getting tired of simply being told they should become missional and take part in the new missional agenda of the church.

Meanwhile, a white couple who had been part of the church in its glory days retired and moved closer to the church building. They immediately began a small group that decided they wanted to reach the neighborhood. Mary began going onto the main street to talk with shopkeepers about how the church might help them. One shopkeeper unceremoniously told her to leave and not come back. Shaken, she shared with her group what happened. As they prayed, God gave Mary a new imagination. Each week she and her husband, Jim, went onto the main street with garbage bags to pick up litter. They did this for a year as people watched and then began to nod at them as they went by. Twelve months later the shopkeeper who had told Mary to leave invited her in for coffee. A conversation began between a retired, white, middle-class churchgoer and a Black-American shopkeeper that then extended into the community, and out of that relationship a coalition of people emerged who walked the neighborhood to see what was happening. They saw the state of homes and the needs of families. As they learned to listen to one another with trust, there emerged a plan to develop housing. This is not the story of a church with a program to reach the community through its building; rather it is the story of Christians living in and with the people of their neighborhood so that the gospel changed everything.

5

We're Not in Kansas Anymore

Missionaries in Our Own Land

Everywhere we go people tell us that the church has changed, something has happened, and they can't keep doing church the way they have in the past.[1] A pastor and mother in Indiana sent Alan a note full of pain. She had been a faithful minister in her denomination for many years but was now struggling with the whole thing. Her son had moved to British Columbia and now had nothing to do with the church, finding it utterly irrelevant to the issues of his world. Wherever we travel we meet more and more Christians who have walked away from church life in practically all its forms. Whether it is traditional, seeker, emergent, or whatever is no longer the point for a growing number of people. They sense we are living in a different world and that their church experiences don't connect with the huge issues of life that they face.

Conversation #1

Reconsidering Our Context—
The West Is Now a Mission Field

At a wedding recently Alan sat beside a woman in her midforties who has been a faithful Mennonite almost all her life. She is not a radical by any stretch of the imagination; she's an accountant, a careful, balanced, and fairly conservative human being. With tears in her eyes she told Alan: "I can't do it anymore. I wish I could. It's not about Jesus or my faith, I just can't deal week after week with the irrelevance of church. So I have left." We share these stories not because we believe these people have got it right but because they illustrate that we are in a new landscape. We are like Dorothy in the land of Oz; we are no longer in Kansas. The church of the West is no longer engaging the huge transitions and multiple, clashing narratives in its culture.

Most of us know the statistics that reveal an exodus from the church. We don't need to repeat here the losses shaping denominations and the aging of the church. Church systems engage the missional conversation because they are scared and looking for a lifeline. Across the continent people are telling us that their church organizations are approaching a tipping point where local churches won't be able to afford full-time, seminary-trained pastors. The confusion, stress, and anxiety are high among many full-time leaders who have been in the job for more than ten years. As one pastor said recently, "I love the church, but I see where it's all going, and I don't know what to do at my age, because if you're trained for ministry, there isn't much else you can do!" Kansas? Not even close.

Some counter this data from the perspective of the megachurch phenomenon. There are more prominent churches of 5,000, 10,000, and even 20,000 people, which might lead us to think the church is playing a more significant role in the culture than we are willing to admit. One megachurch pastor even interviewed the presidential candidates. But you can't build a future on this model, because just from the perspective of leadership, these megachurches are created by people with leadership gifts that few have. To see this model as an answer is to tell 98 percent of churches and their leaders that they have no future. But the issue is not whether a pastor can get a prime-time spot on television, how many churches are shutting down, or the percentage of pastors who are leaving the ministry. We are in a new world; we no longer live in Kansas, and the church as we have known it has to become very different in order to journey in this new place.

The Canadian Catholic philosopher Charles Taylor calls ours *a secular age* in which our "present condition is to say that many people are happy living for goals which are purely immanent; they live in a way that takes no account of the transcendent."[2] People's primary concerns are about success in this life (the immanent); they rarely ask questions about that which is beyond (the transcendent). At the same time, people are now feeling terribly insecure about the social, political, economic, and environmental realities of our world. Witness the recent financial crisis and the corresponding stress it created the world over. People go to church looking for words of security, a place of sanctuary. They look for a spiritual enclave, which is only natural, but this is the problem. Churches have chosen to give people what they say they want: a place of danger-free solace, escape, and comfort. But the church is called to be what they really need: a foretaste of God's new creation, a movement of people who change the world, not escape it. In the midst of all this transition, a missional church is formed by people who are starting to own that they are no longer living in a safe place—like Dorothy's Kansas—where the church has a clear position in society and the gospel is a commonly understood message. Just as Dorothy had to learn to navigate Oz differently than Kansas, we too must learn new skills to be missionaries in this new place. What does it mean to be in this new place, and why do we put so much emphasis on place and neighborhood in this book?

Place and Space

Central to the biblical story are place, concrete land, and everyday experiences on that land. To have a spiritual experience with the God of the Bible is to encounter him in concrete reality here and now. When Jacob dreamed of God coming down to meet him, he built a stone memorial, which became a sacred place for Israel that shaped its imagination. We are not suggesting we do this again. What we have lost in modernity though is this sense of the importance of place. When the Benedictine Order was formed, one of the vows a monk took was not to move on to some other place. Behind this imagination was the conviction that God is only known in the particularity of place and time.

Jesus came and *pitched his tent* in the neighborhood. He was located in a geography that wasn't incidental to his message or ministry. All of this has changed in modernity, where place is increasingly irrelevant. We even have some gurus telling us that with the Internet *place* is no longer important—we can meet people anywhere at any time in the virtual world. We are keenly aware that most of these gurus write this kind of romantic nonsense from some very nice locations and are unwilling to move to more uncomfortable environments. Place does matter. We do not see escapist enclaves where biblical characters have spiritual experiences that do not deal with reality. This is nowhere clearer than in the promise of land. Abram was promised a place, and God's promise was for a concrete reality. Abram was not called to leave Ur so he could have a spiritual experience. He was called to leave Ur for a new reality in an actual place. And although he never saw the complete fulfillment, the promise remains. As Revelation states, a new heaven and new earth will be established as a concrete place for God's people to realize his promise (21:1).

This kind of *place spirituality*, though, is hard for most of us to imagine. We have been shaped by a *space spirituality* that is founded in the rootlessness of modernity and postmodernity. In that world-view, mobility and anonymity are essential so that individuals can re-create themselves in empty space without accountability or authority. In space spirituality there is little need to recognize anything concrete or historical. In this space we can have private, individualistic experiences with God, and the church's primary job is to promote such experiences. In this space there is hope of ultimate freedom without coercion so that people are free to determine their own identity and are free from any concrete sense of community or roots. With space spirituality there is little need to understand our context.

Place spirituality, on the other hand, helps us recognize that we live in a territory that is full of history, meaning, heartache, and joy. Jesus was incarnate in a concrete time and place in history; he was not an abstract, cultureless being in some kind of spiritual space. And today the Spirit is leading the church back into the neighborhood, into concrete territories to recognize what God is doing there.[3]

What Kind of Place?

Until recently the church held a central place in the culture. In some respects it still does. Those running for political office have to roll out their religious credentials, but most of us understand that this kind of pantomime doesn't shape their decisions or actions. This is especially true for growing numbers within younger generations who face a profoundly insecure world that is in crisis on many fronts. It's not that these young people don't want to be formed in a Christian way of life; it's that it all seems profoundly irrelevant to the issues they are facing personally and globally. Drive through the midwestern states and you'll notice two things in small towns: tall silos and beautiful church buildings. The architecture tells you that when these structures were built, the faith they represented was central to the life of the towns. Church buildings were constructed to symbolize the prominent role Christian faith played in public life.

Over the last half century Christianity has been progressively disestablished. In a pluralized and globalized world the position of the church has changed. Varieties of voices, cultures, religions, and mores compete for recognition. Consider the fact that the average person in America watches at least twenty-eight hours of television per week. Much of it pumps information, stories, and opinions into people's imaginations that shape how they see the world. We are naive to think the church can compete with these stimuli through three songs and a thirty-minute sermon or a drama and a worship band. Internet, chat rooms, blogs, Facebook, and iPhone are the mediums and the message shaping the imaginations of North Americans. YouTube has a more powerful effect in shaping people's interactions than a Sunday series or a small group Bible study. The world is shifting radically; the Christian story has become one option among many others.

This is a relatively new development for which most of us are unprepared. Until the early 1960s a broad-based Judeo-Christian culture informed our society. Stanley Hauerwas and William Willimon penned what has become a classic book, *Resident Aliens*, in the late 1980s, in which they wrote:

> Sometime between 1960 and 1980, an old, inadequately conceived world ended, and a fresh new one began. We do not mean to be overly dramatic. Although there are many who have not yet heard the news, it is nevertheless true; a tired old world has ended. . . . [In the past] Church, home, and state formed a national consortium that worked together to instill "Christian values." . . . A few years ago, the two

79

of us awoke and realized that, whether our parents were justified in believing this about the world and the Christian faith, *nobody* believed it today. . . . All sorts of Christians are waking up and realizing that it is no longer "our world."[4]

At the end of the first decade of the new millennium, huge numbers of Christians are now wide awake to these new realities. At the same time, most churches operate with structures designed for a time when church was firmly at the center of life. Leaders are still trained to resource this form of church, but the culture has shifted. What was germinating beneath the surface has grown and foliated into a full-blown transformation so that attractional churches are falling like tired, browned leaves shaken loose by the winds of change. We are at the end of an era. The deep roots of a churched culture are being pulled up and discarded along the roadside. South African theologian John de Gruchy put it this way: "Western Europe and North America may not be going through a social crisis in the same way South Africa is, but they are not less societies in crisis. Their crisis, which is largely the result of rapid secularization, is . . . the collapse of values and meanings which had somehow given society its sense of cohesion in the past."[5]

Those of us inside churches (all kinds, not just the so-called *traditional*) have invested a lot into church, and we know we have become quite adept at leading these forms of church. We have grown to be comfortable with the processes that once attracted people to our events, but we are recognizing now that we don't live in such a world any longer. A missional church is no longer satisfied with being a provider of spiritual products; our national and global crises are just too big. We have to become missionaries in our own contexts and be God's catalyst for a new future. Part of this means identifying strategies that cannot take us along this road.

Irrelevant Strategies

Before proposing ways of becoming missional, we must deconstruct strategies we know so well that prop up the illusion of an established church at the center. These strategies may have been effective in the past, but in the new space they misdirect.

80

Flawed *Church and Culture as Congruent*

This approach assumes that the church is still basically an integral, formative part of the larger contexts in which members find themselves, and so there is little cultural or translation difference between the world and language in the church and that of its context. While we may know our contexts are going through massive transitions and the ways most churches have been formed no longer reflect this change, the habits of church meetings (e.g., small groups) and outreach (evangelism) reveal how hard it is to let go of established patterns.

One church Alan visited announced that the leadership had planned an event to reach the community: a big street sale to connect with their neighborhood. At one level it was not a bad idea in terms of understanding a community—most of the church members simply drove in on Sunday or midweek—but it completely missed the changes in demographics, attitudes, and values in the neighborhood. So much of our evangelism is shaped by the conviction that the values and beliefs of the context are just the same as those of the congregation. The primary symbols and terms of meaning (e.g., *righteousness, morality, progress, domination of nature, effectiveness, spirituality,* and *success*) are assumed to be virtually identical both within and outside the church. The church perceives itself as both part of and representative of the society with its presumed role of shaping the private, moral life of citizens. This is simply no longer the case.

Our traditional assumptions are quite straightforward: we live in a basically Christian society, therefore evangelism is about individuals knowing Jesus personally. In the last century, architectural and program evangelism illustrated this assumption. A church building, pastor, and congregation were planted in a new housing development along with programs for youth, mothers, men, and so on. The assumption was that the people in the development, like those coming to the church building, just naturally went to church or were ready for the programs. A *construct a program and they will come* imagination guided strategies of evangelism. This is exemplified by a young pastor in the Midwest who said these were the expectations of his people, but they found that the neighborhoods around the church were filled with people who would never dream of setting foot inside a church. It is a new day.

In the past there were three basic reasons churches grew. The most basic reason was sex. People married and had lots of babies. People still marry, but they don't have lots of babies anymore. Furthermore, many of those in the church are too old to have babies. The second reason was that people were loyal to the organizations they joined and stuck with them through thick and thin. Those days are gone! Finally, there was once a time when the rhythms and demands on people's lives were much less than today. This allowed them to spend a significant amount of time as volunteers in the church. Churches grew for these reasons, but the conditions for these elements are gone for good. We are in a different world.

A visit to congregations reveals the changed context. They are increasingly populated by graying empty nesters and grandparents. Pastors are at a loss about what to do; they were trained, as good generalists in nationwide franchises, to run programs for loyal members. Some churches still reproduce the old strategies by selling their property and moving to new developments to lure in a new crowd. Others hope that by improving what they are doing (contemporary or emergent programs) they will attract new people.

Recently some of Scott's retired friends shared how their Bible Belt church is struggling with its future. The majority of the members are retired, but their new pastor is bringing some new life back. This church is in an established neighborhood, so he wants to expand parking, build a new fellowship hall, and update the existing building. While the members are enthusiastic about having a new venue for fellowship, some question the financial commitments required. The problem is that nothing about this imagination even remotely considers the shifting context of the neighborhood, which is now primarily Hispanic. The pastor wants to lead this church back to a pattern that was shaped for a context that no longer exists.

Church Renewal as Mission

In response to the crisis of the church's loss of place, certain renewal theologies sprang up in the late twentieth century that put forward the assumption that if we get the internal work of the church right, this will fix its malaise.[6] There was also a lot of emphasis on what is called church "health" programs.[7] *Church renewal* morphed into *church health*. Just as Oprah has regular conversations about personal physical, emotional, and social health, so a whole group of processes emerged through which a church could check its health on the assumption that if you worked on the health issues then the church would reengage its context in mission. Enough time has passed to show that this is patently not the case; we just get more focused on ourselves in a different way. The belief that internal renewal or health leads to missional life is false.

Each strategy reveals a common assumption: if a church attains health in the proper proportions, then it will be effective. Book after book describes how to renew worship, recover a biblical understanding of leadership, liberate the laity, release spiritual gifts, or form community. They all address in-house (internal) matters of style and structure (rooted in a New Testament pattern). But they also reveal two common misconceptions: (1) Their contexts are neutral, so we can apply a common, neutral set of renewal or church health strategies into any context whatsoever—apply the formula and the world will beat a path to our door. (2) It assumes that looking at one's inner life results in mission. Neither assumption is true.

Third: Church as Presenting the Answers to the Culture

An assumed congruence of values, beliefs, and language between a local church and its context results in assuming we already know what will reach people in our context. We don't really need to listen to them, and we only need to figure out the right marketing strategy. This way of thinking is at the heart of most evangelism strategies that are based on a redesigned scale in which we are supposed to locate a particular group of people on the scale and so know what they need to hear. If we use this method, the result is that instead of listening to others and entering their world, we treat them as objects for outreach.

Recently an executive of a denomination was pulling his hair out over the decisions being made in the national office. They had received an estate worth over 20 million dollars. Of that amount, the national office had spent 10 million dollars hiring an agency that researched people's attitudes toward the denomination and then developed a massive marketing campaign that included chat rooms and a bobblehead dog mascot. The executive was frustrated because of what this program suggested—namely, there was nothing wrong with the church's perspectives, and all it needed was a marketing challenge on how to attract more people into what was already there. Nobody and nothing on the inside needed to change; it was about how to present and market who they were. This is the attractional mind-set that has to die before a missional imagination can be born.

In a pluralistic society *God talk* doesn't make any sense to those outside the church. People are asking questions about life and God differently, so we should not assume we can put the answers in nicely boxed sound bites. No one wants our easy answers to their difficult questions. They long for honest dialogue with someone who will actually listen to their story and engage their narratives.

A Missional Strategy

A missional strategy is shaped through dialogue and engagement with the contexts and neighborhoods in which we live. When Scott assumed his role as the community pastor at a church in Saint Paul, Minnesota, one of the first things he recognized was that mobilizing people into small groups was central to the life of the church. This was not the typical megachurch full of middle-class white people; because of its unique location with the suburbs on one side and the inner city on the other, the congregation was ethnically mixed. But his concern was that most of the people in the small groups were suburban, middle-class white people. As Scott looked at the ways that churches do small groups, he realized that the majority of small group churches were suburban, middle-class, and white. As he listened and learned what was happening in their neighborhood, it became obvious that a monolithic small group strategy was not the answer. They needed to spend time entering the lives of the people in their neighborhoods, engaging their stories, and then ask questions about church structures and strategies that would best serve the people of the surrounding communities. Classic small group scenarios were not the way of missional life in this context.

Successful missional life in one context may be an utter failure in another. Even when shifting from one neighborhood to another within the same city, the way we go about being God's missionary people will change. Missional engagement is not homogeneous; there is no one-size-fits-all pattern. Instead we must enter the local community and sit with the people to enter and be shaped by their narratives in order to ask the question of what God may be up to in that context. This is about getting outside the walls of the church and leaving behind our assumptions about what people need to attend to what is really happening among the people in a neighborhood. To be very blunt, this is not a matter of buying demographics and studies that tell you about people; it's about entering their lives, sitting at their tables, and listening to the way the Spirit is inviting a new imagination about being church in that context.

The life of the church must be changed through renewed dialogue with Scripture and by letting Scripture speak to us through a serious dialogue with the cultural context. This is a process we call "engaging the context," in which the people of a congregation recognize the changing character of life and the need to reenter the particularity of their neighborhoods and communities so that the gospel can become alive in that situation.

Engaging the context speaks to what Paul meant when he said, "To the Jew I became like a Jew. . . . To those not having the law I became like one not having the law. . . . I have become all things to all men so that by all possible means I might save some" (1 Cor. 9:20–22). The early church engaged its context when they presented the gospel to its own diverse, pluralistic society. The task of the local church in our present situation is to reenter our neighborhoods, to dwell with and to listen to the narratives and stories of the people. We are to do this not as a strategy for getting people to church but because that is how God comes to us in Jesus, loving us without putting strings on the relationship. It will be in these kinds of relationships that we will hear all the clues about what the Spirit is calling us to do as the church in that place. But this is not a strategy we take *to* a context; it is a way of life we cultivate *in* a place where we belong.

One of the first things a missionary to our own culture does is stop to listen to and enter into the stories of the people in order to understand how the culture actually functions. He or she reads books, listens to and watches the local media, as well as looks at trends, priorities, and so forth. But to be perfectly honest, the real work involves sitting with the people, listening to their stories, and entering their world with an open mind and heart—not bringing predetermined decisions and goals to the table. If we come to sit with them in this way, we replicate what John describes in his Gospel: Jesus came to *pitch his tent* beside ours (John 1:14). When we do this, we will be able to hear what is happening and discern what the Spirit is up to; we will read people through God's lenses and see what he wants to turn these people into.

A local neighborhood is never static; it's always in dynamic interaction with a myriad of other narratives, constantly changing and reshaping its life. Little can be assumed anymore; things change much faster than they used to. Driving down his street on his return from a two-week road trip, Alan saw that three houses were for sale, an old bungalow had been torn down and a huge home was being built in its place, the neighborhood store had redesigned its front with chairs and plants, and his lawn was packed with overgrown grass— and that was just the surface of the neighborhood. Change occurs constantly; little stays the same these days. One way to imagine the changing of our contexts is illustrated in the following figure, which shows a spectrum of change in a culture.

Little Interaction with Other Cultures	High Interaction with Other Cultures
Static Cultures	Accelerated-Change Cultures
Europe AD 500–800	Native Americans after Europeanization
Americas before Columbus	Contemporary North America
Tribal Groups in Borneo	Urbanization of African Tribes

Figure 9

North American culture is far to the right on this spectrum. It is not a monoculture but a set of multiple narratives continually interacting and changing one another. We are in a situation that is much less a context of a dominant narrative story than it is the interaction and clashing of multiple narratives. We create churches and read Scripture based on the assumption that the Christian narrative, if not *the* narrative, lies close to the center. We must now shape a new dialogue with Scripture and our contexts to learn how the gospel might engage our new contexts. Out of this dynamic we will discover what missional life might look like for us.

An example of this is the way in which Anglicans and Methodists in the United Kingdom have developed their Fresh Expressions movement.[8] This missional movement of ordinary people has come out of hard wrestling with their contexts and attending to what's happening in their neighborhoods and communities. It comes from dwelling with and among people.

Local churches that engage their context learn to listen and see where God is at work in the midst of all the confusion, anxiety, pluralism, and technological transformation. This is far more than bringing answers and receiving nothing, leaving the context changed but the Christian unchanged. Instead both are changed through dialogue, and our attention is on what God is doing in the neighborhood rather than in the church. Following are two steps a local church can take to enter and engage in the missional journey.

1. Entering and Listening to One's Context

Each of our contexts is unique; each has its own particular intermixing of cultural interactions. The gospel, therefore, must always be understandable in the language and thought patterns of that context. Specific forms of missional church, therefore, will be constructed locally. The primary need is for local strategies of engagement with the people in the neighborhoods, which is why it is so important for churches to become skilled in listening to their own setting. Missional life emerges from the kind of listening that connects us with what God might be up to in a particular context.

This does not mean a local church should abandon its traditions, values, and language. Without denying its history, a missional church chooses to hold this valued tradition to one side in order to enter into and listen to the narratives of people in the neighborhood. The dotted line in the diagram signifies this willingness to hold one's own perspective in abeyance while first listening to others. This protects a church from proposing answers to questions people may not be asking and guards us from imposing our assumptions before the local people have been heard.

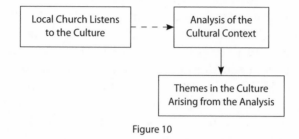

Figure 10

This listening has two parts. First, the church becomes attentive to what is happening through direct involvement with the people in that location. The best way to do this is by entering the neighborhood and hanging out with people, joining community organizations, connecting with people across the street or at the local coffee shop, and taking walks and initiating conversations—doing a thousand little human things that make life rich. It is essential to be in a setting long enough to be known and to absorb its ethos in order to become part of the life of the context, not just an observer.

Mark had spent his life working in churches. He was very good at youth ministry, and as he got older, eventually he was asked to become a member of the church's board. The town where Mark lived was exploding with growth as new housing developments and strip malls seemed to spring up on a monthly basis. Mark and his family kept driving in and out of the community, oblivious to all the dynamics transforming its life. Then one day Mark noticed that many of the kids from the junior high he passed each day were just hanging out with nothing to do. He discovered that the tremendous growth of the town resulted in massive problems for kids because of the lack of opportunities for healthy activities. As he talked with school leaders, community agencies, and kids themselves, Mark was challenged by what was happening to the young people of his community. He knew that no program in his church twenty miles away would mean anything, so he began *pitching his tent* in the community, gathering friends, praying with people, and asking what God wanted to do.

Over a couple of years a community center emerged designed by the kids from the junior high. The kids became involved in the center because someone had taken the time to enter their stories and invite them to imagine ways of living in the town. The other amazing part of this story is how all kinds of people began coming together with Mark to ask new questions about their town. In the midst of this the mayor, who knew Mark was a Christian, finally asked, "Why are you doing this?" The conversations continue, and the meaning of missional life is being shaped in new ways.

A second element of listening has to do with attending to the values and meanings that underlie the surface activities of the neighborhood. This listening is not a technique—it requires time, presence, and a passion for people and place. Computer printouts and demographic profiles are no substitute for a deep, loving, listening presence. When Alan listened to conversations about the values shaping a New Age Mall in the neighborhood of Danforth Church in the late 1980s, they revealed themes of rejection and transformation. These were not obvious on the surface, but the church would have been unable to have a meaningful gospel encounter in that community without grasping these themes. The people's concerns in shaping the mall revealed other values about ecology, community, and a search for the supernatural. It became clear to Alan that people in his neighborhood

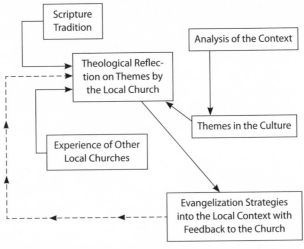

Figure 11

were seeking ways that would reconnect them with one another and nature. This level of listening is a first step in cultivating a missional life. The themes that emerge from this listening become the clues about what the Spirit is doing in the community.

2. Reengaging the Biblical Narratives

The second step of engagement involves asking questions about how our biblical understandings interact with and are being challenged by this involvement in the community. In learning to ask the kinds of questions mentioned above, a local church brings the fruit of its listening in the neighborhood into a dialogue with Scripture instead of assuming it already knows what Scripture has to say. We are learning to read Scripture with the eyes of our neighborhood, which reshapes our imagination about the mission of God and allows us to begin seeing Scripture in a new way. Missional life emerges from these kinds of engagements rather than from trying to sell church programs.

All of this requires considerable commitment to the local, which arises out of an incarnational theology of place. Indwelling in a place and its people doesn't happen instantly; it requires being there for years. Perseverance and commitment are essential. It's not another evangelism tactic worn like a coat and discarded when the next trend arrives. It is a way of life that must form the air a local church breathes. It is an ongoing process—a spiraling dialogue committed to change that requires a constant rereading of Scripture. Churches willing to risk such a life will form missional communities.

6

Why Do We Need Theology?

Missional Is about God, Not the Church

A few years ago Scott was part of a team leading a conference on church strategy. In conversation among the presenters, one of them brought up the missional church topic. Immediately and with quite a lot of emotion, one of the other presenters responded, "Those guys are just theologians who don't know what is going on in the realities that we face as pastors. They have nothing practical to say." The conversation was immediately shut down.

This response has been repeated to us over and over again. We are convinced theology is critical to the formation of missional churches. If we don't think through our theology, then missional just becomes better tactics and strategies for attracting more people.

Conversation #2
Rethinking the Gospel—
The Missio Dei

You are a theologian. This claim might shock you. A lot of clergy don't even think of themselves in this way, much less everyone else. The fact is that we are all theologians in one form or another. We are

91

not all professional theologians with degrees, but we are continually shaping who we are out of our most basic convictions of who God is and what God is doing in the world. Theology is "talk about God," and being a part of God's missional people means that we are speaking about who God is and what God is doing in this world within a specific context. This is theology, at least as we see it. Therefore we must reclaim theology for everyday people so that we can talk about God in ways that fit where we live in the world.

Types of Theology

We need to talk about theology or we won't be able to form missional communities, because missional community is all about what God is up to in the world. Theology must move out of the academic ivory towers and into the local places where we live, eat, work, and do business. Shaping missional life means seeing ourselves as theologians who are learning to talk about God in our local contexts. In his book *Constructing Local Theologies*, Robert Schreiter identifies three types of theology.[1]

1. Community Theology

Theology isn't just for seminarians. To become missional, local church members have to wrestle with the meaning of the gospel in their local context. Schreiter asserts that as the people of a local church listen to those in their neighborhoods and bring these conversations into dialogue with Scripture, their church becomes a place of doing theology because it is asking questions about God.[2] This means a local congregation should consider for itself what the gospel means and how to apply it in a particular place.

Community theology assumes the importance of asking questions we often do not ask. The most basic example of this is the question we keep asking in this book: What is God up to in this neighborhood? Think of what this could mean in communities of socioeconomic and ethnic diversity. It's easy to develop well-intentioned plans for racial reconciliation or social justice without ever having a conversation with a person of color or someone who has lived in poverty. A community theology invites this listening and becomes open to being surprised by God's purposes rather than our good intentions.

2. Prophetic and Poetic Theology

Prophets and poets, as we use those terms, are people within communities who give voice to theology that is emerging from among the people. Prophets challenge community theology where it breaks away from Scripture, and they proclaim with clarity what is arising within the community as a challenge to previously held standards. Poets give voice to the ways that theology is being formed in a local context. Songs, sermons, pamphlets, and testimonies can be poetic expressions of local, contextual theology. The poet has the task of capturing the themes and metaphors about God that are emerging in a local church.

3. Outsider Theology

We all tend toward myopia—reiterating what we already know and not seeing much else. Every denomination and local church tends toward insider thinking. Therefore, while we have to engage in forming local theologies, we will do that best as we learn to stay awake for and open to hearing from those outsiders who can provide contrasting and correcting perspectives. Such outside voices might come from professional theologians; people from different countries, traditions, or subcultures; and even contrarians in our midst. Some of the most constructive input for doing local theology can come from the unchurched. These are the ones who will tell us if we are truly taking the gospel into their context or just force-feeding our own words.

Being a theologian in this missional journey is not about going to people with answers, plans, or strategies; it is about entering into the local context and having conversations. *Contextualization* means "weaving together," and when applied to theology, it is the process of using conversations to interweave the gospel into every aspect of local life. It requires taking seriously what is going on in the neighborhood and reflecting on what the gospel means in those situations. We are not like doctors who prescribe solutions as much as we are like artisans who cultivate possible linkages between local life and the God of mission.

93

what does this look like for introverts?

The Missional God: Jesus as a Contextual Theologian

John tells us in his Gospel, "The Word became flesh and dwelt among us" (John 1:14 NKJV). Eugene Peterson paraphrases this verse, "The Word became flesh and moved into the neighborhood" (Message). John uses *Word* to communicate a radical message: the Word is Jesus and the Word came to earth and showed us who God is. Jesus's way of being a theologian was to embody God in a local setting. He came to earth not in an ideal time, an ideal way, or with an ideal plan. He did not come to all people at all times in some kind of universal way of the mystics or philosophers. He came in a very particular way to a particular people at a particular time in history. He moved into the neighborhood of Galilee and demonstrated there who God is. Hebrews opens with these words:

> In the past God spoke to our forefathers through the prophets at many times and in various ways, but in these last days he has spoken to us by his Son, whom he appointed heir of all things, and through whom he made the universe. The Son is the radiance of God's glory and the exact representation of his being, sustaining all things by his powerful word.
>
> Hebrews 1:1–3

God sent himself; he is his own missionary. He came to open the door for the restoration of all creation. In this coming we see what God is truly like—not a universal principle distant and beyond all. God is transcendent and beyond our comprehension. What is beyond us is the fact that instead of God being a distant principle we must grasp through some form of contemplation or philosophical logic, he comes to us on our level, and he does this in a very specific, *local* way. He "moved into the neighborhood."

When we read the New Testament, we see that almost all of the stories occurred *in the neighborhood*. Jesus came where people lived in their daily, ordinary stuff. He did not wait for the ideal religious time or setting and then ask people to come to him. He went to them. One of the ways he did this was by eating with people. The Gospel of Luke highlights this in a significant way, relating that Jesus ate with outcasts, sick people, sinners, and tax collectors. Around meals he healed, talked about the kingdom of God, and told stories. He entered into conversations and did theology there. This does not mean that his theology was in flux but that theology is contextualized through the dialogue; it is made real as life is shared.

Waking Up and Cooking Meals

Alan loves the process of cooking. He gets up early Saturday morning and either bikes or hikes to a local market filled with produce from around the world. In one area stands a fish store with fresh cod, salmon, mussels, clams, oysters, and on and on. Around the corner are all the smells of freshly baked bread made with some of the most exotic ingredients. His favorite—fig and anise bread—is awesome with fresh salmon grilled on the barbeque. On the other side of the fish market stands a French deli that makes the most amazing pâtés to be found outside of France. People line up six deep to buy their duck pâté to serve for an evening with friends. Just to the side is one of Alan's favorite coffee counters; behind it lie canvas bags filled to the top with all kinds of roasted beans from around the world. He stops to pick up a pound of Cuban—a strong, aromatic blend.

Amid all these aromas and sights, occasional conversations begin as people jostle to get the food. Alan looks about and puts together a recipe in his head out of all the great ingredients that lie before him. After an hour or so he heads home, and by late afternoon he is in the kitchen preparing all these foods, readying them for a great evening with friends. Life doesn't get better than this. It's in these moments that he feels deep inside that this is an amazingly beautiful world God has given us and that there are rhythms and ways one can never sense in the rush of our lives.

Of course the question is, "What does this have to do with theology and being missional?" The answer is, "Everything!" Let us explain. Clemens Sedmak writes, "Theology has been on loan from the people of God to professional theologians for a long time," and he wants to return theology to the ordinary people in local churches. He describes what's involved in doing theology as a process of *waking up*: "Waking up means learning how to listen, learning how to see, learning how to discover, learning how to speak . . . being attentive to the particular circumstances." And this means learning to ask, "How do I awaken to what God is up to in our local context, in our particular time and place?"[3] Waking up as Christians necessitates looking about our neighborhoods in order to ask: Where are we? What time is it? What are these smells and tastes and sounds? What might God be up to in the midst of all this life and energy?

This is where theology begins because it starts with God and the question of what God is doing in the world. If we begin with questions like, "What is a missional church?" or "How do we become externally focused?" or "What kind of church-planting strategy should we develop?" or "How do we form a multisite church?" then we are not asking questions about what God is doing in the world; we are asking questions about the church and about tactics. This is why theology is so important—it keeps pointing us to the questions of God in the local. It asks these questions as if the people in our neighborhoods matter and are more than just the objects of our strategies to get more people inside our churches.

Another image Sedmak uses to describe what he means by *theology* is that of the *creative village cook*. Rather than missional communities buying an ecclesial version of prepackaged, precooked food off a supermarket shelf or from a McDonald's franchise, we are cooks who use ingredients that are present in the local. This cooking attends to what is growing in the neighborhood; it asks what kinds of food God wants to prepare in this place and among these people.

When Jesus fed people, he attended to the needs of those around him. He sought out the food the people had with them (fishes and loaves on one occasion) and served them as a good host. He depended on the people and didn't simply use them as objects for some other purpose. In order to be this kind of cook, Jesus was rooted in the local context and attended to what was happening among the people themselves. All of this is about doing local theology—attending to people in the neighborhood to create with and among them a meal that will celebrate God's life and presence. Waking up and learning how to be a cook in the midst of the local are common, everyday images we want to use to describe the way we cultivate missional life.

Waking Up and Setting Tables in the New Testament

Although examples of this kind of theology abound in the New Testament, we tend not to read it in this way because most teaching assumes the New Testament is about neutral, contextless propositions, doctrine, or moral advice for living. While its pages have elements of these in it, this is not really what is going on in the Gospels and Epistles. We want to suggest that these writings are more about the local theology Sedmak describes than about abstract doctrines or moral advice. We think the New Testament has a whole lot to do with how people were trying to work out the meaning of God's big story in the midst of all the local issues, tastes, and sounds of their neighborhoods and communities rather than principles and absolute propositions for all times and places. They understood themselves as sent to "gossip" and communicate the Good News of Jesus in the midst of their neighborhoods and communities. The kind of preaching we do today isn't found much in the New Testament. We have taken this wonderful concept and turned it into something that happens from the front of a church on a Sunday morning, usually given by a person with a seminary degree, or we assume that it must involve having a formal speech ready to give people if they ask about our beliefs.

What has happened, of course, is that we are now living with some two thousand years distance from these people. A lot has changed. A simple illustration demonstrates this. Most of the time in these documents when a New Testament writer uses the pronoun *you*, it is meant in the plural. For example, at the end of the letter to the Ephesian churches when Paul calls upon us to "put on the whole armor of God" (Eph. 6:11 NKJV), our tendency (default) is to interpret this as a personal call to each individual Christian because we have come to read everything individualistically. In the passage, however, the word *you* is plural and so is addressed to a whole community. Because we live in a very different world, we need some assistance to make the translation.

The New Testament is about ordinary men and women waking up to their neighborhoods and figuring out how to be the kinds of cooks who set the gospel table using local ingredients. Let's look at an illustration of this in Paul's letter to the Ephesian Christians. It

97

is usually assumed that he wrote this epistle to various household churches in Ephesus as well as a number of other cities up the Lycus Valley (in modern-day Turkey), such as Colosse and Laodicea. Our intention here is not to spend a lot of time providing background information about these places, but it is clear the Christian message had created conflicts and confusion among new believers in this area as people struggled to make sense of the gospel in the midst of multiple other stories and claims about the way to find truth or God. Paul wrote this letter as a means of addressing some of these issues and as a way of assisting young Christians in discerning the truth. He did the same with the Corinthian church to the south in Greece. There the issues were quite different, so Paul's letters took on a different subject and tone. The point is that Paul was doing local theology; he was helping people in Ephesus awaken to what was happening around them as well as ask how God might be calling them to shape their lives in that context.[4] A good example of this is found in the opening paragraph where Paul writes:

> He made known to us the mystery of his will according to his good pleasure, which he purposed in Christ, to be put into effect when the times will have reached their fulfillment—to bring all things in heaven and on earth together under one head, even Christ.
>
> Ephesians 1:9–10

We have been trained to view these words, with their language and meaning from two thousand years ago, as though Paul were teaching abstract doctrine in a university or seminary and wanted to ensure that everybody crossed their t's and dotted their i's. But these words are actually wonderfully local, missional theology. Briefly, here's why: The clue is in the word *mystery*. Philosophers and other teachers traveled up and down the Lycus Valley telling people they had found the key to the *mystery of life*. They claimed to have the formula or secret knowledge that would answer the big questions about the mystery of why we exist and the purpose of the world. Therefore anyone who was aware of what was happening would have realized that these teachers were seeking to win adherents. And many young Christians were confused by all these claims and counterclaims.

You may have gone onto the Internet to get some information (Alan seems to constantly be looking up recipes on the Internet). Suddenly a window pops up telling you there are five secrets for losing the spare tire around your waist in less than two weeks. You click on this wondrous offer only to discover you have to pay money to obtain the secret that will transform your life and turn you into a man with a thirty-two-inch waist or a woman who can wear a size two. The message, in other words, is this: with a bit of cash you can join the chosen few who have discovered the mystery of the good life. This was the kind of thing going on in Ephesus and along the Lycus Valley, and it was confusing people.

So Paul addresses this real situation in his time and place by answering the question: What is God up to in the world, and what does it mean in this place at this time? This is the central missional question. Awakened to his neighborhood and wanting to set the table of the gospel, Paul picks up on the word *mystery*, knowing that people were really wrestling with these questions. He tells the Ephesians:

> Look, there really is a mystery about ourselves and the world. We all know that. We see how these questions of why this world exists and what we are meant for create huge anxiety among people. These "philosophers" make their money preying on the anxieties and fears of people in our community, pretending that they have the secret and we have to be initiated into this secret by them.
>
> Well, here's the really good news! Here's the kind of table God has set for us all if we want to hear it. The real mystery about the world has been made public in Jesus—it's not a little secret that only a few can have. In Jesus, God is now making public that from before the beginning of the creation he was already at work on something huge.
>
> Everyone knows the world doesn't hold together as it should. We have walls of division. We are torn apart and alienated from one another—just look at the hatred between Rome and its occupied countries, or between slave and free, or between men and women, and that's just for starters. Well, God's secret purpose is now out in the open for everyone to see: in Jesus God is in the process of bringing the whole of creation back together into one healed and renewed community. That's the mystery, and it's now out in the open for everyone

99

to see—not just for a secret few with the money or insight, but for everyone. And here's the amazing good news: in our neighborhoods and communities this new people—the *ekklesia* of God—are called to be the sign, the witness, and the foretaste of where God is planning to take the whole creation in Jesus.

Ephesians 1:9–10 (our paraphrase)

Paul and the other New Testament writers were continually doing this kind of theology. They were not trying to be abstract and difficult. They were awake, listening to their neighborhoods and the communities where these little households of God were springing up, and they kept asking, "What kind of table does God want us to set in the name of Jesus in the midst of these particular sounds, smells, and sights?" This is why theology is so important: it keeps making us begin with and stay with these questions of what God is up to in the neighborhood. When we don't learn to practice this kind of theology, we will keep defaulting to church questions and find ourselves asking how to become externally focused or plant churches or be multisite or whatever and just assume we already have all the answers to the questions of what God is doing in our neighborhoods. Being missional is about doing local theology—waking up to our context and becoming God's wonderful cooks with all the flavors and aromas of the local.

7

God's Dream for the World

What Is a Contrast Society?

God has a dream for this world. As we saw in chapter 2, the kingdom of God is central to the biblical perspective of what God is doing in this world. Mark 1 tells us Jesus proclaimed that the kingdom of God was present with his coming: "The time has come. . . . The kingdom of God is near. Repent and believe the good news!" (Mark 1:15). The kingdom of God was opened up with the coming of Jesus the Messiah, and God's dream for the world was revealed through him.

In Luke 4 Jesus explains the nature of this dream:

> "The Spirit of the Lord is on me, because he has anointed me to preach good news to the poor. He has sent me to proclaim freedom for the prisoners and recovery of sight for the blind, to release the oppressed, to proclaim the year of the Lord's favor." Then he rolled up the scroll, gave it back to the attendant, and sat down. The eyes of everyone in the synagogue were fastened on him, and he said, "Today this scripture is fulfilled in your hearing."
>
> Luke 4:18–21

God's dream for the world is about the redemption of all creation, not just individuals getting into heaven; it is about the restoration

101

of life as God intended it to be; it is about realigning life around God and God's ways.

Conversation #3
Reimagining Church—
Sign, Witness, and Foretaste of God's Dream for the World

The third conversation that flows into the missional river is the call for God's people to be a sign, witness, and foretaste of this dream for the world. Missional is about embodying God's dream, even though we do that in an incomplete manner. It is a dream that has begun but is not yet fully manifest.

Sign, Witness, and Foretaste

In past generations the sign of God's activity and life in a town or city was evident in the form of architecture or the identity of clergy. When visiting a city in Europe or looking at the skyline of a North American city or town, we see that church buildings were designed to communicate something significant about God and the meaning of salvation. The steeple, the cross, and the elaborate architecture of church buildings communicated both God's greatness and his purposes. The North American scene inherited a poor man's version of this same stream of thought. For most people today, these signs are cultural vestiges—interesting historical landmarks that no longer speak to our souls.

A sign points to something else; it calls attention to something that cannot be readily or directly seen. But architecture was never intended to be the primary sign of God's dream for the world; his people were to be that sign. The biblical scholar Gerhard Lohfink uses Israel as an example of what the church is called to be:

> Foundational to an important strand in the tradition of Old Testament theology is the idea that God has selected a single people out of all the nations of the world in order to make this people a sign of salvation. His interest in the other nations is in no way impeded by this. When the people of God shine as a sign among the nations (cf. Isa. 2:1–4), the other nations will learn from God's people; they will

come together in Israel in order to participate, in Israel and mediated through Israel, in God's glory. But all this can happen only when Israel really becomes recognizable as a sign of salvation, when God's salvation transforms his people recognizably, tangibly, even visibly.[1]

This call to be a sign, witness, and foretaste of God's dream is a call for us to be a contrast society. In the early centuries of the church, Christian bishops wrote letters asking Christians to stay in their cities or towns when disease broke out and care for the sick rather than be like the Romans who ran away to save their own lives. Soon the Christians were known by a story of attending to the needs of others rather than caring for themselves first. This made them a contrast society, and as such they lived God's dream for the world. In modern times we have stories such as that of the doctor in Edmonton who began cutting the lawns of people in his community. This story illustrates how one family started to live out God's dream in their neighborhood (see chapter 4). They were a contrast family and as such drew others to God's dream. A contrast society is a people shaped by an alternative story, living by a set of distinctly Christian practices.

Contrast Society

Being a contrast society has not been a common expectation of churches in the West. Because we have assumed the wider culture is primarily Christian, the church's influence has been relegated to that of the private, internal life of the individual. We have lost the call to a salvation that not only saves us *from* sin but saves us *for* life the way God meant us to live in the first place. As a result we don't usually conceive of salvation as being a process of becoming God's people who practice the way of life that he intended in the midst of the mess of the world. Since the church's influence has been relegated to private matters of the individual's soul for so long, we have no voice to speak to a way of life that is practical and embodied in the everyday. In too many cases talk about God, the church, and salvation has to do with issues that are lifted out of life. If missional is a call to be part of a contrast society, what will that look like?

Shaped by a Contrast Story

The shape of our lives is not determined primarily by the application of good sermons or even good theology, new ideas, or structures like small groups. All of this has very little actual impact on the conduct of our everyday lives. Rather, we are shaped by stories.

The headline read: "It's Not the Diet, It's the Dieter." The point was that the real determining factor in the ability of a person to change the way he or she eats is not the diet book with all its good advice but the inner stories a person has about himself or herself. The internal story is what determines how one acts. If I believe I am fat or in need of indulgence or not likable, then I will live out that story in how I eat. For example, think about a man who is a workaholic who knows that his life pattern is impacting his health, sees how it undermines his family, and knows it is less than pleasing to God. He may feel a degree of guilt, and he may have privately confessed his sin to God, but none of this addresses the source of the workaholism that is driven from inside by a story about who he is or should be. Stories shape who we are.

The American story about a country founded as "a nation under God" determines how Americans see themselves and respond to others. Gordon Cosby, who has been the pastor of Church of the Savior in Washington, D.C., since the 1940s gave his final sermon on December 28, 2008, at the age of ninety-one. What has shaped Cosby and the church in the amazing work they have done is the conviction that the story of God's dream for creation become reality in their city. In Seattle, Karen Ward and her urban, monastic community live out God's story in their neighborhood. In the same city, Tom and Christine Sine provide hospitality to people from all over the world as they live simply and seek to shape a community around God's story. In Philadelphia, Shane Clareborne and his community live out God's dream among the poor. Their story is shaped by the conviction that God's story calls them to live in a place and never move. In Toronto several years ago Jason was in his late thirties and making a huge salary on the stock market. He sensed this story was shaping his life in ways that would deform his picture of the world. So Jason and his wife left their high-paying jobs on Bay Street in Toronto and began working with marginalized women on the streets of Vancouver. Today they work with others seeking to release women in other parts of the world caught up in sex slavery.

An endless, tangled list of stories shapes our lives. The gospel invites us to enter an alternative story shaped by the mystery, memory, and mission of God. Theologian Barry Harvey offers a way of seeing the Bible as God's "travel narrative":

> The Bible provides nothing like a map that charts the precise path for us to follow into the future. What it does give us is the travel itinerary of God's people, that is, the story of their pilgrimage as strangers and foreigners through this world toward the kingdom of God. . . . An itinerary, by contrast, consists of a series of performative descriptions designed to organize our movements through space: "to get to the shrine you go past the old fort and then turn right at the fork in the path."[2]

One can't really understand a travel itinerary without actually getting out and walking the path, whereas a map can be comprehended without ever going anywhere. In other words, instead of providing a specific map for us regarding what it means to be God's missional people, the Bible invites us on a journey where we figure out what it means as we walk. We actually become a contrast society on the journey. This means we need to start some experiments of journeying.

Throughout the history of the church we discover local communities shaped by practices of life that cause them to stand out and cause others to take heed. They have learned to live as a contrast society shaped by hospitality, radical forgiveness, the breaking down of social and racial barriers, and self-sacrificial love. As we live inside God's story, we are shaped into habits of life that empower us to be the sign, witness, and foretaste of God's dream; it becomes our travel itinerary. For some this will be in homes. For others it will be public spaces like coffee shops. And others will use their traditional church buildings, but most likely in unique and unexpected ways. Whatever specific forms take shape, when God's people adopt God's practices, people outside the church will take notice.

Contrasting Practices

Most of us need some basic steps to get started, and the Scriptures offer specific practices that can help us become a contrast society. These practices are not a list of principles or uniform formulas for missional living; they are organic, flexible rhythms that will be practiced in different ways in different places. In chapter 15, for example, we will talk about how to practice hospitality as a way of living out this travel itinerary. To be a people of hospitality today is to stand in contrast to a very inhospitable world. We live in a culture controlled by fear and isolationism. Engaging people in the neighborhood with conversation and inviting them into your home will stand out in significant ways. There are, however, many different ways to actually practice hospitality in our world. In some neighborhoods, inviting strangers into your home would be met with immediate rejection because they don't know you well enough. An appropriate initial act of hospitality might be to get together for coffee or make a concentrated effort to talk with people as you see them on the street. In another neighborhood, it might be better to set up a basketball goalpost and play ball with the latchkey kids after school. The form hospitality takes will depend upon the nature of the context; there is no one-size-fits-all pattern.

This is one of the reasons we cannot provide a specific list of characteristics for the missional church. The way a church is a contrast society in a wealthy suburban area will be quite different from the way a church is a people of contrast in an under-resourced neighborhood. In the coming chapters we will propose a set of practices, manifest in many different ways, that can form us as a missional people.

How Practices Work

Practices are not a to-do list of items to be checked off one by one. They are more like the work of a musician practicing his instrument, an athlete training for a competition, or a craftsman working at his skills—they are about living inside a way of life. Practice forms us into who we become, the embodiment of the stories that shape us. In Scripture we find all kinds of practices that shaped God's people, without which they no longer looked like God's people.

To see this in a different way, imagine yourself as a citizen of first-century Ephesus, a city that is only about three miles long and two miles wide. Houses are built right next to one another, and streets are very narrow. A man named Paul and his companions arrive, and they visit the synagogue. Paul teaches, and people witness miracles. Then a riot flares up because an idol maker is losing business due to people turning to Jesus (see Acts 19). It is impossible for you as an Ephesian citizen to be ignorant of what is going on with Paul and his band. While they have done things that have gained specific public attention—public healings for instance—you have also been able to see some things we today consider a part of the internal part of church life that reveals the nature of the God they worship. You have observed their prayers, communion, miracles, and relationships with each other. You can hear their singing, their talk about God and how Jesus changed things. The architecture of the city allows anyone with questions to see the reality of what it means to be a follower of Jesus. Their entire life together is visable, a sign of God's life. This is what we mean by all of our life being missional. We cannot cordon off our outreach practices and make those public while withholding the private ones from view.

The practices we propose are not new, but the last twenty years have seen a revival of interest in them. The work of people like Richard Foster, Dallas Willard, and Eugene Peterson has helped us see the long tradition of spiritual practices that have formed God's people throughout church history. At the same time, we are emphasizing something slightly different. In most cases people read about the spiritual practices and apply them as individual disciples. While we don't believe this is the intent of authors like Foster, Willard, and Peterson, we do see how the individualistic nature of discipleship in the Western church has caused us to see practicing the disciplines as a private matter for those who are serious about their faith. In fact, some books on this topic include things like accountability and community and corporate worship as options from which individuals can choose—usually after listing individual disciplines like prayer, fasting, and journaling. In a couple of recent books on various prayer disciplines, the authors use numerous examples of individuals who benefited in private from the practice. The dedication and self-discipline of individuals to these practices is important, but this individualistic way of approaching these disciplines most often falls short of the goal.

Along with personal disciplines, a contrast community seeks how spiritual practices can be promoted and lived out within community. Instead of viewing community itself as a discipline for individuals, it is rather a context in which we practice faith. For instance, Brother Lawrence's classic, *Practicing the Presence of God*, points to a way of communing with God on a constant basis, whether it be while peeling potatoes, dropping off the kids, or meeting with colleagues at work. Individuals might read his little book and see its value and even make a plan to implement it. But it is much more likely to become a habitual practice if a group of people commit to doing it together, to talk about how the practice is developing on a regular basis, and even to be in daily contact to remind one another of the practice. Although this specific discipline is personal, it need not be private. And when we learn to practice these disciplines together, we are much more likely to do them in a public way so that others can see them as a sign.

Three Sets of Missional Practices

The first set of practices that demonstrate how the church is called to be a sign, witness, and foretaste is the practice of *presence*, which highlights the specific things that mark God's people as those who relate to him in a contrasting way. It includes disciplines like worship, experiencing God's presence, connecting with and listening to God, simplicity, sharing the Lord's Supper (communion, the Eucharist), and keeping the Sabbath. To most who are reading this book, these things will not be new. We simply want to bring attention to the fact that being God's missional people begins with God and how we relate to him through his Son in the power of the Spirit. The Scriptures make it quite clear that God created man and woman to walk with him (Genesis 2) and that his intention was compromised by sin. Therefore God has called his people to a mission to relate to him in a unique way in the midst of a fallen world.

This is much more than an encouragement to have an individual devotional time. The missional question that leads to the experience of contrast is: How do we do these things in community? In other words, how do we do them as a people together? As stated above, the spiritual disciplines that are so crucial to being formed by God's presence have long been highlighted as personal practices. While this is good, it means that most of the time the spiritual disciplines are left to those who are very committed or are prone to be somewhat contemplative.

By contrast, the Bible emphasizes spiritual disciplines for the community. Fasting, for instance, is most often spoken of as a corporate act. Keeping the Sabbath is more than a personal choice; it is a way of life for a community. But the way to develop practices that connect a group to God's presence cannot be prescribed from the top down or from a centralized leadership; the desire must arise from those who are seeking to live out the mission in their everyday lives. There are great resources available to help a community wrestle with the answers and experiment with various alternatives.

For instance, a group might commit to working through a common prayer guide, such as *The Divine Hours* by Phyllis Tickle. Each week people could come together and share what they experienced in this process of praying and reveal what they sensed in their communion with God. This is just one example of a specific way of practicing God's presence; there are many others. Another example is a small group in that has embraced the discipline of the Daily Examine, an ancient practice where individuals review their day and look to see where God is at work. When they talk with each other, they ask where they saw God. They know that left to do this practice alone, it will often be skipped.

Any specific practice is intended to promote an experience with God. At least it should be. The point is the experience of God's presence, not simply performing some ritual for the sake of getting it done. Many Westerners are not comfortable with this because God's presence is full of mystery and unpredictability. We find it easier to perform a ritual we can control and measure, so we evaluate how many times we attend a church meeting or register how many devotionals we complete. But the practices are not ends in themselves, and if we think of them as such, they become a distraction from the real goal. *God's presence* is what marks God's people as his own, and the practices are there to facilitate this encounter with the mysterious, wild, relational God.

The practices of *love* comprise the second set, which speaks to the ways a group of people commit to do life together. These practices include things like having five to ten people form a primary community in which people can take off their masks and be safe with one another, commit to working through conflict even if it gets messy, learn how to build up each other with God's empowerment, and practice a clear initiation process through baptism. Such practices require a group of people to have some serious conversations about how they will be in one another's lives. The life of the missional church cannot be done by a conglomeration of individualists who see each other only at formal meetings. Being missional means that we do life together in a way that marks us as distinct from the surrounding culture. How this happens specifically will depend upon the people involved, but again, these are not questions that can be answered by the leadership at the top. Instead, the leadership must facilitate conversations about these practices and provide ways for people to discover how to move into them.

In community we learn to love one another, and through the journey of learning to love we are formed and shaped by God through the others in a group. One of the common struggles found in churches is how people deal with the inevitable conflict that occurs in relationships. In the wider culture, relationships tend to be somewhat disposable, and therefore, when conflict arises, it is not uncommon to move on to the next relationship. Sadly, too many relationships today are nurtured only as long as there is mutual benefit to the individuals involved. An essential piece of being a contrast society at this point in history is the ability to deal with conflict in a healthy and constructive way. Unfortunately, this is not currently a strong point within most churches. Most people have not been equipped to communicate through conflict and deal with the issues that arise in the process. Churches that actually expect conflict and talk through how they will respond to it are much more likely to work through the issues than those that don't.

Many times people remain present but disengage and fail to deal with issues they face. Some even call such behavior loving, but deep down resentment builds. For the most part this is the pattern of the world, not of God's contrast society. What does a church have to offer a neighborhood (as spoken of in chapter 5) if the people within the church community cannot apply the gospel to themselves? Where is the forgiveness? Where is the freedom to make mistakes? Where is the opportunity to accept one another in weakness? The practice of love will be messy—relationships always are—but when the neighborhood sees a group of people working through such messes, it will be a powerful sign of God's dream for how the world should be.

The third set is the practice of *engaging the neighborhood*, which is the focus of chapter 5. A church will engage the neighborhood in the same way it lives before God and with one another. If we live as a contrast society in how we relate to God and others, the neighborhood will see this. But if we do not, our attempts at engagement will be ineffective because those who supposedly have something to offer the world actually have nothing that looks any different from the world. But when a church loves God and one another in a way that a watching world can see, it is able to go into neighborhoods and enter into conversations about what the gospel means in respect to the many difficult questions that we face today.

Part 3

COUNTLESS
MISSIONAL
JOURNEYS

8

The Journey Ahead

Following the Winds of the Spirit

Remember *Where's Waldo?*—those wonderfully colored picture books with dazzling images of animals and exotic places. On any given page of a book were five or six images of Waldo, but they weren't obvious. You had to look hard to find Waldo, but once you began to know what you were looking for, spotting Waldo's location started to get a lot easier. In some ways missional church can be like looking for Waldo on one of those pages—it requires adjusting how we see the church. At first it seems hidden, but then we see it, and it makes sense.

Now that we have introduced what the missional church is and why it is so important during this specific time in history, we need to discuss what it entails to become a missional church. We are on a journey we can't control, and we would really like to have a map with well-marked directions. This is a journey through a new country, a place we have never been before. That is why it feels like we are looking at a *Where's Waldo?* book. Our instincts are to listen to the first voice that says, "I know where we are! I've seen this before! I have the formula (or plan or strategy); follow me!" What we have to do is stop for a bit, gather ourselves, and become attentive to our surroundings. This stopping and suspending the need for answers will

115

help us hear what the Spirit is saying in this new place. We believe this journey will be shaped by ordinary people as they enter their neighborhoods and communities and see what God is doing.

It's not a journey toward some ideal or vision of the church but one of encountering God in the ordinariness and messiness of local churches in this new place. As a result there will be as many manifestations of missional life as there are churches that embark on the journey. But we can learn from others and how they got started. Let's see what this might involve by looking at how others went on this journey.

Don't Go without the Presence

Exodus 33 tells the story of Moses's encounter with God. He is at the beginning of the immense journey of leading God's people through the desert—a new clearing for Israel, a place they have never been before and don't recognize. Moses is fearful and needs assurance and some mechanisms for controlling and managing the challenge of leading these people. After more than four hundred years of slavery, their training as brick makers and their slave mentality will never suffice in this new space no matter how much they are dressed up in new language.

Moses is in a situation beyond his skills and abilities. Egypt had molded Israel's imagination that didn't disappear just because they crossed the Red Sea. Seeking the certainty of God's presence and wanting a way to gain control over the situation before him, Moses asks to see the face of God. But God tells him that no one can see his face and live—the certainty of God is beyond what any human being can face. Instead God covers Moses's face with his hand and then walks in front of him so that Moses is able to see his back.

Like Moses, we have also entered a *clearing* where we feel vulnerable and are searching for ways to control the unknown. We want a map or, better yet, a GPS. In this clearing we are brought face-to-face with God. In the desert clearing Moses sought to manipulate and control outcomes by trying to manage God, but he knew that he had to begin with God. At the same time, he had to learn that God would not be manipulated or managed; to be present with this

116

God was an utterly different thing—it was to be in a place where one does not have control and can't determine the maps.

Moses's experience with God follows an encounter in which the Lord declares he will not go forward with these people. He says he will send an angel before them to drive out their enemies, but his presence will not be with them. The reason for this is what happened during Moses's earlier absence on the mountain. The newly freed slaves were terrified; they were far, far outside their safety zones and familiar boundaries that had defined the rhythms of their lives. All the familiarity of Egypt had been taken from them. They were encamped in a desert clearing, and their leader had disappeared on a mountaintop. So they did what their past experience told them should be done—they built something to represent God in some way. They created a tangible image of something familiar that would stand in their presence as protection, because they surely needed protection at that moment. In the desert clearing they defaulted to the habits and strategies of Egypt. Who would have acted differently?

When Moses finally descends from the mountain, he knows they have defaulted to their old habits; Egypt is deep in their imagination. Moses returns to the mountain to reason with God about his role with these people. He is terrified by the implications, and he says to the Lord:

> You have been telling me, "Lead these people," but you have not let me know whom you will send with me. You have said, "I know you by name and you have found favor with me." If you are pleased with me, teach me your ways so I may know you and continue to find favor with you. Remember that this nation is your people.
>
> Exodus 33:12–13

Moses is bargaining with God. He is putting it in the face of God: "Look, you are the one who called me to lead these people. They are your people not mine, so don't beg off now in this terrible moment." What is so amazing about the Hebrew Scriptures is that they don't pretend or try to create some polite ideal of what is happening. Moses is terrified! He's out of his depth and fearful of God's response. The worst that Moses expected occurs; God has said that he will not go with them (Exod. 33:3). So Moses bargains for his own and these people's lives. He argues with God:

If your Presence does not go with us, do not send us up from here. How will anyone know that you are pleased with me and with your people unless you go with us? What else will distinguish me and your people from all the other people on the face of the earth?

Exodus 33:15–16

Moses, in desperation, risks arguing with God by saying: "Please, see what has happened! You brought these people, these slaves, out of captivity, and if you don't go with them now, they will be destroyed and your reputation will become a laughingstock in all the earth." The only thing that distinguishes these people and makes them unique is that out of all the people on the earth, God chose to go with them. Without God's presence the people will be just like every other nation, so they might as well join in with another nation and live like they do. God finally relents: "I will do the very thing you have asked, because I am pleased with you and I know you by name" (Exod. 33:17). Moses understands the situation (this clearing); in this place the old tactics of Egypt won't work. In the clearing the primary issue is that of discernment and learning all over again how to listen to God.

In our clearing we are asked to discern what God is seeking to shape even though all our instincts are to turn back to our default settings to make things work and control the outcomes. In this clearing we have to let go of our need for manageability, predictability, and control in order to listen to the God from whom new things emerge. This is how missional life develops. Our choices are between discerning God's presence or defaulting to predetermined goals, vision statements, and strategies. We need to follow Moses's example—he had confidence that God was present in the journey even though he had no maps of this strange territory.

Understanding the Ways of the Spirit

Moses asks of God, "Teach me your ways so I may know you and continue to find favor with you" (Exod. 33:13). He knows that in the desert it is essential to learn a way of life—habits and practices that will change this people from slaves and brick makers into God's

118

people in the Promised Land.[1] Similarly, our missional journey calls us to learn habits of listening and discernment.

Around us are many quiet stories of people who have learned this way of life. When Gordon and Mary Cosby began missional experiments four decades ago with the people of the Church of the Savior in Washington D.C., they didn't know what it would all look like. One thing they did was buy a farm about thirty miles from the capital to create a retreat center. Wellspring became the place to which members went regularly on silent retreat and prayer to listen to the Spirit in the midst of continually changing challenges. They formed mission groups and trained everyone who came into the church how to listen to God in practices of discernment. One of the critical acts of discernment members of each group had to do was ask about the shape of the mission to which God was calling them and then present this to the church. The list of creative engagements in mission in the community around their headquarters is amazing. No one at the beginning of that journey could have imagined the development of a hospital or the rehabbing of derelict tenements so that they became places of hope and dignity. The Cosbys would never have used the word *missional*, but they are a shining example of a missional community.

Chris Erdman at University Presbyterian Church in Fresno, California, invited the members of his church to pray, listen, and discern some of the ways the Spirit might be calling them into their community. One of the results was members of the church entering the apartment buildings around the church and discovering ways to be accepted and welcomed by the many Hispanics living there.

Pernell Goodyear in Hamilton, Ontario, saw the plight of the poor in the lowest socioeconomic zip code in Canada and moved from his suburban church plant into the neighborhood. Others joined him and moved into the neighborhood, and they listened quietly to the people of the area and sought to know what God wanted to do in this new place. The outgrowth of this is The Freeway, a Christian community with an amazing collection of stories of people being shaped by God in the midst of urban poverty.

In Lincolnshire, United Kingdom, we met Dr. Pete and Cath Aitkins, who have joined with others in imagining what will be involved in replanting local churches all over that area of eastern England. We went with Aitkins to a place in the countryside where he often walks and listens to the ways the Spirit might be calling in that small, rural area where the churches are dying. Aitkins took us up a dirt road between two farmers' fields. About halfway up and about fifty feet off the road stood an old stone church that was quite small and no longer used. On this site four or five hundred years ago was a tiny chapel where each day the abbess of a nearby order prayed for the mission of God in the area. In the early spring and late fall when the fields are fallow, it is possible to see, etched into the ground, the outline of a medieval village that had sprung up around the chapel and the nearby abbey. The abbey is no longer visible, although a short drive reveals stones from its ruins that a casual passerby would never notice. Aitkins describes how in his long prayer walks he knows the Spirit wants to do something like this again across his beloved Lincolnshire. He doesn't have road maps in this place, but he discerns that God is up to something in the neighborhood, and that energizes his life. These and so many others are witnesses to a way of being God's people in this new clearing, listening to the Spirit asking what God is up to in this new place.

A basic conviction of the Pentecostal and charismatic movements of the twentieth century was that Christians are people who are shaped by the life and work of the Spirit among us. This insight was a gift to the church. But our sense is that this reenergizing of the church affected its inner life without really influencing the ways in which the Spirit shapes the church for a missional life. Structures and programs remained essentially untouched, and a fundamentally attractional model of church went unchallenged in most cases. We are not arguing for charismatic gifts or expressions, nor are we seeking to disagree with them. In one sense, we don't think that is the point. We are arguing that in this new clearing we have to learn again how to attend to the ways the Spirit is seeking to form us as mission-shaped people in our neighborhoods and communities. If a local church does not get this, it will only see mission as one among numerous other programs that make it successful and more attractional.

Sailing with the Winds

We find ourselves in much the same situation as Nicodemus in his encounter with Jesus in John 3:1–8. As a Pharisee, he was a leader in the Jewish community who assumed he knew the ways of God, but he went to Jesus at night with a sense of confusion and consternation. It was clear to Nicodemus that Jesus performed the signs identified with God, but he needed to understand what was happening and where he might fit into this himself. Jesus responded by telling him he must be born again. Another way to say this is, "You need a new imagination." Jesus was saying that the rules had to change and, therefore, Nicodemus's understanding (imagination) was missing what God was actually up to through the presence of Jesus.

Jesus responded to Nicodemus with the words, "The wind blows wherever it pleases. You hear its sound, but you cannot tell where it comes from or where it is going. So it is with everyone born of the Spirit" (John 3:8). The missional way is about discerning the winds of the Spirit. How do we make sense of this metaphor? In sailing, the crew focuses on how the winds are blowing and then works the sails to capture the winds. But the crew has no control over where the wind will blow. On the missional journey the challenges are the same. We can't manage and control the Spirit, nor can we assume we know where the winds of the Spirit are blowing in this new space. We are sailing on a vast new sea where we will need to understand how the currents of mystery, memory, and mission can direct us.

The church is not driving a motorboat with control over direction and destination. The motorboat can move in a neat, straight line. A large church in Florida opted for the motorboat strategy after their strong senior leader was captured by the missional vision. They passed out books, created a new plan, and expected all programs, staff, and laypeople to align with the new missional *motor* driving the church. They then began making changes to turn what had been a successful *attractional* church onto a missional course. Within a few months, after some initial effectiveness and excitement, people felt manipulated and driven into something they did not understand. While they understood the concepts, they had not been invited into an imagination; they were simply shown a new map of where the motorboat was now heading. The experience of sailing, on the other hand, involves learning to trust the winds of the Spirit rather than a GPS system. In sailing God teaches us to attend to the ways of the Spirit.

Through Whom Does the Wind of the Spirit Move?

Our rock-bottom conviction is that the Spirit of God is among the people of God. By this we mean that the Spirit is not the province of ordained leaders or superspiritual people; instead the Spirit is in what we call the ordinary people of a local church. Furthermore, we don't mean that this requires people to become like the super-spiritual. Instead we mean that the Spirit is actually at work in our ordinary, common lives. This means that God's future—putting into action God's dream for the whole world—is among God's people. At one level this may sound obvious. It's not! When choosing among politicians or entertainers or when selecting a new pastor, we look for someone out of the ordinary—someone who is bigger than life. This is not how God is creating a new world. God works among ordinary, everyday men and women.

Very practically, a missional church is formed by the Spirit of God at work in the ordinary people of God in a local context. A practical implication is that this imagination changes the focus of leadership. Rather than having plans, programs, strategies, and goals, they ask how they can call forth what the Spirit is doing among the people. When this happens, the potential for discovering the wind of the Spirit is exciting. We now turn to a practical process that will call forth what the Spirit is doing.

9

Starting from Here

Where Is Your Church Now?

Any journey begins from here. Right here—wherever *here* might be for you. You don't start a journey from where you wish you were or where you hoped you would be.

Where is your *here*? What is happening among your people in the places where they live and work right now? What are the stories shaping them at this moment in time? The missional journey begins where people are, not from some vision for where we would like them to be. Visioning and radical language about what the church should be are of little help; in fact, they create barriers to entering this journey of catching the winds of the Spirit. In order to begin where we are, we have to take the time to attend to and listen to the narratives and stories of our churches and our people. Usually when a leader comes with a vision or plan, he or she is not in a place for listening to the whispers and narratives of people. This section examines some ways we can come to say, "We are here."

What Is the Spirit Doing in the Church?

To begin with, the conviction that the Spirit is among the people of God is not positive thinking or wish fulfillment; it is a conviction about how God is present both in the world and in our experience. What we find, however, is that leaders often confess this in theory, but the looks on their faces reveal something different. They feel that the people of their local churches are closed off to any sense of what God is doing, they are resistant to innovation, or they are simply satisfied with the status quo and not ready to dream any dreams.

Leaders still believe that if this missional journey is to happen, they will have to come up with a vision and plan and then try to sell it all to a board. The imagination of many leaders is that the Spirit is at work in the church but only among a small number of people with ideas and initiative who know how to think outside the box and see a different future.

All of this points to the fact that our churches are social systems. The local church we belong to is shaped by a history that forms the ways it works and how people interrelate. These social systems tell us how to behave and what roles and rituals are appropriate for people inside the system.

When Alan attends church near his home, he sees a social system that has grown to depend on a pastor doing just about everything from the front and a lot of people who love having him do it (especially the children's story) because he is young and charming and has a quaint British accent. This church, if Alan has read the Sunday bulletin correctly, has programs people can join and a board that makes most of the decisions and then communicates them to the members. It is formed around a social system with rituals that shape how people behave when they are together—the time services begin, the way the worship band opens, the length of the worship section, the use of small groups, coffee time after the service, communion once per month, outreach programs designed by the pastor and board, and so forth. These social systems are powerful shapers of a group's life; they determine how a group understands church in terms of roles, what should and shouldn't be said, and how people should behave. Unless we understand a local church as such a social system, we won't understand why it often is not a place where ordinary people imagine that the Spirit is up to something through them. The social system determines how people act and what they believe is possible. Figure 12 will help you understand where you are.

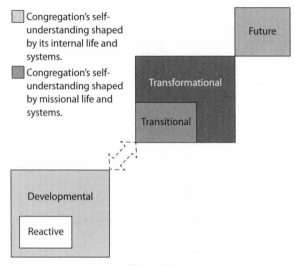

Figure 12

The diagram suggests four ways of reading how a local church as a social system perceives itself that can help it answer the question: Where are we now as a church? But this is not the whole story. Later we will discuss how to listen to the stories of the people in any kind of local church in order to invite them into a place where they can hear the Spirit. At this point, however, we want to look at a way of saying to a local church: You are here! This kind of locating will assist them to begin talking about the implications and start to ask new questions about discerning what the Spirit is saying.

This diagram is not intended to tell people they are in a right or wrong, good or bad place; nor is it intended to tell people they need to move from one to the other. If we use figure 12 as a way of chiding the people of a church or telling them they have to change, then we will shut down the chance for conversation. The diagram is simply a starting point to talk together about where we find ourselves. This kind of conversation can invite people into the missional journey and encourage them to risk talking about going into places where they have never been before.

There are four ways to understand a local church as *reactive, developmental, transitional,* or *transformational.* No church is purely one of these four; it is always an amalgam of each. We can, however,

125

ask which description best fits our church at this moment. But we have to be careful in doing this. We are not trying to define or label a church; we just want to mark where the people see themselves now. Because the Spirit is among the people of a local church, there is hope and there is a future. Let's now discuss what each of these elements means.

Reactive

Churches usually begin with great energy and expectation. A number of people with a big vision work their hearts and souls out seeding and cultivating a new church. They often live close to each other in the community. But over time this dynamic changes. The church tends to get more focused on its internal life, and the surrounding neighborhood goes through demographic changes. Often the members of the church and the local community grow more and more dissimilar.

Alan was called to an old, downtown church in a large city. When it was founded around 1910 it reflected the people of the neighborhood. Slowly different types of people moved in. As the children who grew up in the church and its neighborhood became adults, most moved out to other communities and either joined other churches or had to drive in to the old church. When Alan arrived, the church had declined to about thirty aging members. They had good fellowship with one another from years of being together, but when they looked out on the street where their church was located, all they saw were strange faces and all they heard were strange languages. The people in the church knew everything had changed; no one needed to convince them of that fact. They didn't like what they saw because it all looked and sounded so different from their experience, and they didn't know what to do with the "foreign" people who had moved in and taken over the community. The social structures of the church members and the ways they reflected this in the building spoke loudly about their fears and anxiety as they felt their world being taken away from them. All the windows were covered in wire mesh, and the huge oak front doors were solidly locked. Around the corner on the side street was a second entrance, and to gain access one had to ring a bell and stand in front of a peephole so the person inside could see who was standing on the step before opening the door. The members had circled their wagons. They were huddled together inside the building, having decided they would care for one another and resist or ignore all the change about them. Their hope was that some nice young minister would come with a young family and restore things to the way they had been thirty years before. *Reactive* describes a church that knows much has changed but decides it will turn in and protect itself from what is going on outside.

Developmental

A developmental church believes it can grow and reach people in the new space by improving on what it is already doing. This attractional perspective focuses on producing programs and content that attract people to the church. The social system inside the church is one that assumes most of what they are doing is right but it's just not being marketed well. In other words, this is a social system that doesn't see the need to question its assumptions and ways of functioning. The developmental church believes the issues of mission and ministry are solved by improving and building on the basic paradigm out of which it already operates and doesn't even recognize its assumptions until they are pointed out.

How to Use This Tool

A great way to use the tool provided in figure 12 is by introducing it to various groups in the church. Explain each of the four sectors and then divide your meeting room into four quadrants representing each of the four elements. Then ask people to go and stand in the quadrant that best describes where they see their church at this moment. People will be standing in each of the quadrants, but the majority will gather in one or two.

Invite the participants to look at where they have all placed themselves and then find someone from another quadrant and discuss why you each chose that particular sector. After this has taken place, bring the group back together and ask them what they experienced and learned. Ask them how their conversations led to new discoveries.

This is the start of learning to listen to the Spirit through others by creating a space where people are given permission to talk to one another about how they see the church at this moment in time. This ability to talk with one another is critical to the process of listening and discerning what the Spirit might be about in your church.

A church in a booming town on the East Coast recognized that the neighborhoods around its building had changed dramatically. It wasn't so much a major ethnic shift as it was younger families moving into the area. The same thing had happened thirty years before when the current church members moved into the then new housing development with young children and babies. Their children had grown up and moved away. The church members thought that the new batch of young couples was going through the same cycles earlier generations had gone through and so the same programs would work with them. All they needed to do was clean up the building, get new people running the programs, and put a worship band up front. What they didn't understand was that the world had changed over those thirty years and young families were very different; they didn't come to the church the way previous generations of young families had.

The church sensed something had shifted and wanted to reach out to people in the neighborhood. What they did is fairly standard; it was a *developmental* approach in which they worked hard at improving what they were already doing. They spent a lot of money upgrading the building to make it more attractive to outsiders. They put in new carpets, gave the place a paint job, and hung religious art on the walls. They spent a lot of money buying a demographic study of the community and decided to begin a new Sunday service. Alongside the traditional 11:00 a.m. service, they offered a contemporary service at 9:30 with a worship band and overhead projection of all the music and Scripture. They started using drama in the service and shifted the sermon series from expositional preaching to sermons on themes like "How the Bible Helps to Make Your Life Work," in which each week a new Bible text was used to give practical helps on the people's current needs and concerns. They worked for several months with a marketing group to develop new brochures with high-quality paper and images that would communicate the kind of people they were as a church and why others would want to join with them. Finally, they decided to hire a new youth and children's worker who would provide high-quality programs.

If they had asked for an assessment of these efforts after a year of working at them, it would have been quite straightforward: the church had grown; there were new families coming to the church. The reality was, however, that these new people had switched from other churches in the area to take advantage of a better children's program and music more to their taste. As for the families moving into the neighborhood—they continued to spend Sunday mornings biking, hiking, or catching up on weekend shopping. They didn't consider church to be a priority.

In many cases, the developmental church can appear highly effective. In a large city in one of the mountain states, Alan was invited to speak at a new, large church out in the first ring of the suburbs. As he drove in early Sunday morning he saw the huge building from the highway with its large parking lot. As he walked in he saw the welcome center and the high-quality brochures advertising the church's programs. But as he casually talked with people between services, it became clear that people transferred here from other churches because of the programs being offered. These Christians were driving a distance to get to the kind of church they wanted. Developmental churches attract people, but they usually are not engaging the neighborhoods or the changed realities of their contexts.

In the diagram, *reactive* and *developmental* are coupled together to show they are integrally connected as social systems—they are shaped by a common perspective about how the church should function in this new space. But the two types are not the same. Reactive churches are usually quite small and in the midst of a downward spiral; they are living off their past. Developmental churches, by contrast, can be very large with lots of energy and multiple, well-staffed programs. The point is that both work out of the same set of assumptions: (1) Their basic framing of the church and what they are doing is right; it only needs to be improved. (2) The church's energy is directed toward continually developing ways of attracting people to its center. The next two categories in the diagram indicate a different kind of imagination.

Transitional

A church in the transitional phase recognizes that no matter how much it improves what it's doing, no matter how attractional it becomes, the context has changed so much that people won't come anymore. *Transitional* implies being in between. It describes a church discovering that it has to get out beyond its own walls.

The work of this transition must be approached carefully. It does not involve changing structures and programs or reorganizing the roles of leaders and boards. As we will show, it begins by assisting people in the church to listen in fresh ways to one another and to the Scriptures before inviting them to listen to what is happening among people of the neighborhoods where they live. It involves learning to ask different questions. Rather than asking, "How do we attract people to what we are doing?" we need to ask, "What is God up to in this neighborhood, and how do we need to change in order to engage the people who no longer consider church a part of their lives?" This is a radical shift in focus; it's a different way of thinking about being the church in a community.

Transitional churches are coming to understand that they don't automatically know the answers to these questions. They are also discovering they cannot figure them out by sitting in rooms discussing the issues with each other, nor can they find the answers by purchasing demographic profiles. These churches suspect the programs borrowed from somewhere else and conferences put on by gurus who tell them what to do aren't going to work. Transitional churches are figuring out that they have to do this work for themselves in their own contexts. They are learning to experiment, by trying new things, failing, and trying again. And they are breaking through the fear-of-failure syndrome. This means they are slowly creating a different social system in their church as they shift away from experts, leaders, and programs and instead move toward empowering one another. These churches don't have to look like they have everything together. The ordinary people are discovering it is their stories that provide the clues to what the Spirit might be up to among them. By being invited to live into their stories and listen to the stories of others, they are learning how to sit with friends and neighbors to *listen them into free speech*. All of this is messy and experimental. Some in the church will become anxious because it feels out of control; they want to reemphasize the existing programs and structures because that was the social system that provided security and predictability. But a transitional church knows it is on a journey in a new space where it will continually be learning rather than simply improving on what it has always done.

130

Transformational

After a period of experimenting, failing, learning, and experimenting again, a transitional church discovers that, like missionaries in another culture, if they are to be a witness to what God is doing in the world, they need to focus continually on engaging their changing contexts and the people of their communities. They know they will be continually adapting to the communities and people where they live. It is not about being trendy or catering to the culture but about being missionaries in their neighborhoods, shaping the gospel in the forms and language of the local people, and remaking church structures and social systems around the context rather than abstract notions of church drawn from a previous point in history.

The journey from attractional to transformational is a huge challenge for several reasons. For example, many churches are fixated on how to bring others in without fundamentally challenging or changing who they are. This is why the attractional model remains the most prevalent form of church life. In addition, there is still resistance to the fact that our culture is in the process of radical transformation in which more and more people are moving away from any desire to have a church as part of their lives. We may be saddened by this reality, but it is increasingly the case. As we become more multicultural, shaped by a plethora of stories other than the Christian story, the church is losing the place it once occupied at the center of people's lives. We have entered a new space—a missionary context. Attractional churches will still reach Christians looking for a better place to have their needs met, but only as they transition into this new space will they become missional.

The Future

Local churches are comprised of good and faithful people who want to develop a mission-shaped future. They have been told that the way to do it is through a strategic plan that will help them design a preferred future. They have been told it is about taking assessments of their current health and then improving on what they are already doing. Such plans and assessments are supposed to help them bridge the gap between where they are now and where they want to be. These methods assume we can manage the future and, therefore, preplan and control preferable outcomes and determine the directions in the space where we find ourselves. It is an illusion that ignores the need to listen to the winds of the Spirit.

The following chapters look at how to begin the journey from a developmental through transitional to transformational church. It will involve journeying into unknown territory. But anyone who has fallen in love, started a new career, or birthed children knows that in the midst of the scariness, a whole new world is discovered that is far more than just an improvement on the old one. Those of us who have had children know that this journey looks nothing at all like those carefully designed plans we had for our children. The world just doesn't work that way. If you are ready for this journey, the next chapters will show you how to enter into these new waters.

10

The Missional Change Model

Getting There from Here

A few years ago Alan purchased a windsurfer to take on vacation. He bought and studied a book that explained how to tie the knots that were needed to rope the sail. He initially tested his balance and footing in shallow waters close to the beach. Finally, after a few hours of this experimenting, he decided it was time to set out across the lake. But he was unprepared for what happened about two hundred yards from shore. Suddenly the wind picked up and grabbed the sail, almost pulling him over. He was racing across the lake feeling like an expert. After about fifteen minutes of undiluted joy, he reached the other side of the lake. Then Alan tried to return to the side where his family was camping. Climbing onto the board, he aimed it toward his destination, but the wind caught the sail and flung him into the cold water. Undeterred, he climbed back on the board, hoisted the sail, and turned the board's nose to the beach on the other side. Again and again and again he was thrown into the water. In the midst of all this exertion, he was getting tired and very cold. Anxiety was creeping into his attempts as he sensed he was losing this battle to make the board go where he wanted it to go.

Alan assumed he needed to control the board to go where he wanted it to go. It was only when he felt fear inside and exhaustion starting to grip his body that he knew he had to do something completely counterintuitive to his command-and-control approach. He had to let the sailboard go with the wind, and this meant going in a direction away from the camp he so desperately wanted to reach. On that exhausting day Alan learned the skill of tacking into and with the wind.

If following the winds of the Spirit is like sailing, we need to develop the skill of working with the wind. We can try to control the journey and force our way toward an assumed destination, but we too will fail to make progress. Tacking is counterintuitive—moving away from a destination in order to move toward it does not make sense. But so often this is the way of the Spirit. One way to work with the wind of the Spirit is to understand the process of change and how people move through the process of adopting new ways of doing things. When you understand how change works, you are able to join in that process instead of working against it.

The Model

Over the last decade we have struggled to understand how change actually takes place.[1] We knew it wasn't in a straight line, nor was it the result of a plan developed by leaders. It was clear to us that change emerged from among the people themselves, so we wanted to create a process that would empower this kind of transformation among ordinary people in a local church. By giving people a way to practice change in this new space, we would be creating the tools for the missional journey that provided a way for catching the winds of the Spirit.

The Missional Change Model is the result. It is the product of over a decade of work, interacting with hundreds of churches in many parts of the world. We created it to help churches learn a bottom-up process of innovation that takes seriously the conviction that the Spirit is among the people. We have used this model with many congregations and are convinced it helps churches move forward on the missional journey. We have seen its power to achieve the kind of imaginative shift—a movement into a new space that few other tools are able to accomplish. Of course this system is one way, and not the only way, into the missional journey.

The basic model is presented in figure 13. What we plan to do here is walk through the five elements that comprise the stages of innovation any group must move through to effectively negotiate a set of new realities they have not engaged before. This is the essence of the missional journey. Because it involves learning to listen to the Spirit in a new space, we need to understand some of the basic elements required to do this kind of journeying together. Some of you reading this book will be familiar with the experience of seeing the changes that need to be made in a church because of the new space in which we live only to have your explanations and proposals resisted or dismissed. In seeking to explain why change needs to happen and in giving proposals for how it can happen, well-intentioned leaders may fail to grasp the basic issues of innovation and how people actually move through a journey of choosing a different way of being God's people. The model explains why this is the case and how to invite people into the journey.

The five elements of the model represent the stages a local church moves through to enter upon the missional journey. Some will see the diagram and immediately conclude it is very linear and looks like a standard strategic planning process. For this book we are presenting the model on a flat page, which limits it to a two-dimensional diagram, suggesting it is just one more linear planning process. But you will learn that the model is like a set of spirals continually turning back on and interacting with one another rather than a straight-line process in which one moves from *A* to *B* to *C* and so on. Since we are introducing a new tool, we need to explain it in the simplest way possible. We have, therefore, decided to start with a simple, uncomplicated image.

Like learning any new skill or habit, we begin by figuring out some basic steps. When children begin to play the piano, they are given a simple set of notes that they repeat regularly. They don't start with a Beethoven concerto or Bach fugue. They begin by learning the keys and how to use them by repetitively practicing simple tunes (to the point of boredom, our children would say). To develop new habits and skills, they start with rote learning. Only with this kind of repetitive practice do they internalize and make their own the skills they need to play more complicated pieces. When we are in a new space, we have to learn new ways of being in that space in the same way.

If you have never sailed before, it would be foolish to get into a thirty-foot sailboat, hoist the sails, and head out into the deep waters and strong winds. A good teacher first gives you some instruction on land about the way sailboats are constructed, how sails work, and what the tiller is all about. The next step involves sitting in a very small boat with a tiny sail and practicing some of the instructions you have been given. When you step into that little boat, you immediately confront something you wouldn't have anticipated—the problem of balance. The boat is bobbing up and down and sideways in the water. This movement in at least four directions at once challenges the balance of a novice. Many new skills have to be learned along the way—a lot of them unexpected, some that can't be explained simply by writing them in a book or showing a video—so we take simple, small, methodical, first steps. This is what the diagram and the following explanations do.

Remember, this is about addressing the question of how we learn a new way of being God's mission-shaped people in the midst of this clearing where we have never been before. It's about beginning the process of asking how we listen to the Spirit together as a local church to move forward on a missional journey. The illustration of the model in figure 13 will assist you to understand some of the key elements involved in this process.

At first the Missional Change Model may seem to be like learning to climb a set of stairs where we have to go from one step to another

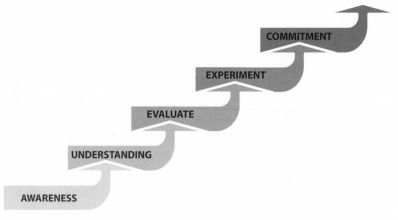

Figure 13

in order to ascend to a new level. Quickly, you learn that it actually works quite differently from that—some people begin quickly with the awareness and understanding stages while others take much more time and are far more cautious. Some of us need to see others test and experiment before being ready to try something new for ourselves. This means that as some begin the journey, others are watching and waiting; then they begin the awareness and understanding stage while others are already working with evaluation and experimenting.

But it is even more complex than that. At each stage we are engaging in new learning and developing new skills, and as this happens we move back and forth across the different levels. Sometimes in the experiment stage we have to go back to do some new awareness and understanding and then move forward again. Just like the process of tacking in a sailboat, it's never a straight line in a single direction but always a spiraling movement back and forth. The skills for doing this develop as we begin with some simple first steps.

A local church starts the journey at the awareness and understanding stages, and there are important reasons for intentionally moving through each stage. Sometimes leaders believe it's easy to introduce change and wonder why we need to move through this kind of process. Our experience shows us that almost every change process (missional or otherwise) designed by leadership (a pastor or board) goes through a predictable cycle. It is accepted by the church with enthusiasm and has initial energy. Some months or a year later it loses this energy and things return to the way they were before the change was introduced. Those involved in church leadership can provide numerous illustrations of programs begun with great energy and fanfare only to dissipate and lose focus after a few years. If missional transformation is introduced as a program or plan from the leadership (a top-down model), it will go through this predictable cycle of energy, enthusiasm, and decline because it was never actually owned by the people themselves.

The Role of Leadership

A key to missional innovation is empowering the people of a local church to discern and develop actions that come from among themselves rather than strategies and programs proposed by leadership. To be blunt, most change plans and programs initiated by leadership will not change the social system or imagination of the people. Leadership has a choice: it can either be in control of plans, programs, and outcomes or it can work at creating the environment that will release the missional imagination that is among the people of God. Leaders need to decide which of these is the most important in terms of being in this new space. The job of leadership is to create the environment in which that can happen, which requires them to learn new skills.[2] This is what the Missional Change Model is intended to do.

How does a new idea or way of living actually enter the culture of a local church and transform their imagination? Just because we have a good idea, great plan, or brilliant strategy for creating the best missional church in the world, it doesn't mean people will accept and incorporate it into their lives. In fact, often the opposite happens. In 1936 inventor August Dvorak designed a keyboard that enabled people to type much faster than they could on a standard QWERTY keyboard (the kind we all use today). By all assessments, Dvorak's invention was a huge improvement over the QWERTY keyboard. It seems logical to expect that new typists would have been trained on the Dvorak to take advantage of the speed and to avoid the damage that can occur to hands and arms from constant computer work. But the QWERTY keyboard remains.

The point is simple: just because someone has a good idea, even a brilliant one, that doesn't mean it will be accepted or change the way people think, work, or act. The defaults within us are powerful. Requesting deep change is something like asking a right-handed person to start doing everything with his or her left hand. Because our habits are so ingrained in us, what happens is what we call the *elastic band phenomenon*. We try to pull people in a new direction with new programs or training workshops, but within a short period of time they return to their former habits and practices because they are the ones that have worked in the past. We all grow used to doing things the way they have always been done, and we resist suggestions to change no matter how good they are.

This is one reason why missional language hasn't really changed much of anything in the church. Someone comes along with great ideas, wonderful PowerPoint programs, videos, or Web blogs, but what really happens is that people take these elements and turn them back into their older ideas and practices so that nothing really changes. How then do we change our defaults? How does a new idea enter a group to such an extent that they own it as a way of life? It requires culture change, which is a deeper process of transformation than just reading new books, creating a new program, or putting ideas on websites. People will always thrill to utopian dreams, but it's what comes next that counts: the daily humdrum of ordinary life. We have to know how change and innovation take place in the living of an ordinary life, not in a conference where a guru tells stories and paints a utopian picture.

The Missional Change Model introduces a process for cultivating this level of culture change in a local church or the systems that serve it. Culture change is never achieved through top-down processes; it happens as people are empowered to name their own realities and develop experiments in which they test out new habits and practices. The model is a guide to cultivating a bottom-up process based on the conviction that missional transformation enters deeply into the DNA of a church when it is cultivated as a process from among the people themselves rather than a program from the leadership to the people.

Although leadership in this bottom-up process is crucial, it operates differently than we expect. The leader (whether pastor, clergy, or board) needs to develop skills in creating environments in which the people themselves do the work of discerning and discovering the imagination that the Spirit is giving them for mission. The leader creates space and experiences for others to imagine what the Spirit is calling forth. It is a move away from the people being passive to the people being at the center of the processes of discernment. In his book *Community: The Structure of Belonging*, Peter Block describes one of the primary roles of the leader as that of convening:

> This is not an argument against leadership, only a desire to change the nature of our thinking. Communal transformation requires a certain kind of leadership, one that creates conditions where context shifts:
>
> • From a place of fear and fault to one of gifts, generosity, and abundance

- From a belief in more laws and oversight to a belief in social fabric and chosen accountability
- From the corporation and system as central, to associational life as central
- From a focus on leaders to a focus on citizens
- From problems to possibilities

For this shift in context to occur, we need leadership that supports a restorative path. Restoration calls for us to deglamorize leadership and consider it a quality that exists in all human beings. We need to simplify leadership and construct it so it is infinitely and universally available.[3]

For Block, leadership has three tasks:

- Create a context that nurtures an alternative future, one based on gifts, generosity, accountability, and commitment.
- Initiate and convene conversations that shift people's experience, which occurs through the way people are brought together and the nature of the questions used to engage them.
- Listen and pay attention.[4]

In the five-phase process outlined below, leaders will get a clearer picture of what all of this will involve.

1. Awareness

In chapter 5 we introduced the idea that the West has changed so much that we now live in a world in which it is necessary for the people of God to be missionaries to the West, and this level of change is accelerating year after year. In the midst of significant change when a culture is shifting dramatically, people often feel something is wrong but don't have ways of meaningfully identifying those feelings. It is common to assume that such feelings, tensions, and anxieties provide a sufficient basis to initiate strategic plans or new programs to change the church. This is not the case. In fact initiating such programs in this environment is exactly the wrong thing to do. When we sense that something is wrong, the first step should be to create a space in which people can find the language for their diffuse feelings that things aren't working the way they once did.

All of us need time to find words and images that will give voice to our experiences when we enter a time of confusion or find ourselves in a new space, and beginning with answers and solutions is counterproductive to this process. In the Missional Change Model the first step is to understand this basic reality and create the spaces where people can feel safe to talk about what they are experiencing. The role of the leader is to cultivate these safe spaces and assist the people in finding (but not provide) the means whereby they can name what is happening. People need time and opportunity to work through their feelings to the place of a new awareness, and they need the space to discover language for what is happening in their rapidly changing world. When others provide language in neatly packaged sound bites, sermons, or programs, they deny people the opportunity to discover together the place where they find themselves.

A man who has worked in an organization for many years suddenly finds himself made redundant as his job is outsourced to another country with much cheaper production costs. As he packs his office or puts his tools away, he feels many different emotions—anger, fear, confusion. He also feels a sense of shame that he has failed or let down the most important people in his life. He can begin to feel useless, unable to make a contribution to his community. He might believe he has no ideas to provide others because he feels overwhelmed by forces that seem too big to name or wrestle into a manageable shape. All of this is normal. Many leaders in the church are experiencing these kinds of feelings themselves as the demand grows for them to come up with solutions in a world for which they were never trained. Awareness is about creating the space, giving the time, and creating the safe, welcoming table where these feelings can be expressed as a first step in giving them language.

When we don't have adequate language to apply to an experience, we are literally stuck; it's impossible to move forward. We must not underestimate the power of language; it is one of the most powerful ways we have to make or create reality. A culture is formed when a group of people develop a common language that shapes and defines how they see and make sense of the world. As they develop ways of talking to one another, certain sayings, images, and shorthand phrases become like an inner code for explaining how things work. This can be tested in simple ways. For example, if you live in Australia and then move to North America, attending a hockey game is like entering a new world where the language about the game and its rules make little sense. But the opposite is also true. As a North American traveling in Australia, Alan went to several Aussie rules football games. It was like entering a different world where people spoke a different language to describe the sport. That language made sense to them, but it was confusing and difficult for an outsider to learn.

Language is the way we create worlds; it's what we do to make a culture, whether that is North American culture or the culture of a local church or denominational system. When we suddenly find ourselves in this confusing new space, the language that had worked so well to this point no longer matches the reality around us. We are disoriented and confused. In this new space we need time and processes to help us begin to articulate what we are experiencing in order to develop the language we need to make sense of where we find ourselves.

Few of us will commit to risking a journey in a new space until we have moved through several distinct phases. First, there comes a willingness to own our need to give meaning to these new experiences of confusion, anxiety, and loss. This is the step of *awareness*. What a leader must grasp is that awareness is about beginning where people are, not where we want them to be or where they ought to be in terms of some program or plan. Awareness requires the willingness to suspend our answers and plans to focus on creating the kinds of safe spaces where people are able to give voice to their experience of disorientation. This is a crucial first step. The second involves deepening the conversations about what is happening to people and bringing these conversations into dialogue with the biblical narratives.

2. Understanding

In the second stage people are starting to grow confident that the environment of the church is focused on listening to one another and cultivating safe spaces where there are no subagendas at work. This is a time when the leadership can talk about what is meant by *safe spaces*, and they can share that there are no hidden agendas. They can also make it clear that this kind of listening and giving voice to

142

the people is one of the ways we learn together to discern the Spirit. As people grow more confident that this is, indeed, the shape of their journey together, a new kind of dialogue starts to happen among them. It isn't dialogue about change proposals or programs; it is focused on people talking among themselves about what they are learning, seeing, and experiencing in the new space.

It is important to recognize that in this period people need to deepen their understanding by having the time and space for conversations. Some will be tempted to jump to solutions and go on, but what we want to do in this stage is invite each other to go deeper with the issues, exploring the meaning of what they are learning through their interactive engagement with one another. Leaders can help this happen in a multitude of ways. They may find themselves in informal conversations around dinner tables or at coffee shops as people test what they are thinking and try out their new levels of understanding. In all this process the leaders need to keep the conversations open-ended and ensure that people don't go to solutions and closure too quickly.

Understanding develops out of awareness. People move from a vague sense of things changing and being in a new space into dialogue with others to frame meaningful explanations for the changes they are experiencing. In this process people start to ask each other new kinds of questions that stimulate new forms of thinking. This leads to the third phase in an effective change process.

3. Evaluation

It is only at this third stage that we want to invite each other to bring the kind of dialogue and sense of safety we developed into conversation with the current practices, values, programs, and overall life of the local church. Notice that we don't start with conversations about figuring out what the church is and what it ought to be. The notion that we should start the missional journey in a church by teaching about the essence or nature of the church is to miss how people innovate an imagination. It is not until this point that people are invited to talk about the implications of their conversations in the awareness and understanding steps for the current life of the church. These conversations have been delayed until now because it

143

takes time to create a safe environment, and people won't have real conversations unless they feel safe.

As people enter this stage of evaluation, they will find it is far less critical and negative than they might have imagined. In our experience this is a place of renewed energy as people feel their words have importance in discerning the work of the Spirit. It is in this space that people are ready to risk dreaming a little about what God might be calling the church to be in their neighborhoods. All of this careful work builds support across the church for experimenting with ways of connecting with the community around them. This is a phase of decision-making because the church is now able to choose whether it will move toward or away from the concrete actions of missional life.

4. Experimentation

In the fourth stage we look at how to create some simple, limited experiments that venture into the neighborhood. These experiments come from among the people, and initially they are appropriately simple in nature. This is about inviting people to dream in ways that can give them some early wins after taking risks. This is a big transition for most churches since the default is to assume plans and proposals come from leaders and are put into action by the people. Here we reverse that process in order to invite people into different habits and imaginations.

These experiments are not about wholesale change—that is the last thing we need at this point. In fact, as these experiments are initiated, it is important to keep communicating that nothing is being changed in terms of programs or structures. Experiments involve taking risks, and so they need to take place in spaces of security. This is why we insist that in the process of walking people through the Missional Change Model there be no structural, organizational, program, or role changes in the church that do not help people live into the journey of the new space. People need spaces of security to feel they have permission to experiment, to risk and fail, and to experiment again without betting everything on the results of the experiments.

A young child is willing to take risks and experiment when learning to ride a bike, because Dad or Mom is holding the bike and the training wheels are there to steady the bike. In the context of this security and predictability the child is ready to risk a few yards without the training wheels. Success in those first few yards encourages the child to try even longer times riding the bike without the assistance of training wheels or Mom's firm grip. It is all the security and predictability that creates the environment for risk and experimentation. It's the encouraging words of Dad or Mom when the child falls off that give him or her the courage to get back on and try again. In a similar way, we invite people into simple experiments and risk in missional life while all the time providing security by keeping the regular life of the church basically the same as it has always been.

This is the point when the people themselves begin to own the change; they are shaping imaginations, taking risks, and discovering the Spirit at work in and among them. When this occurs, missional transformation begins to take on a life of its own. Some people experiment, which encourages others to try experiments. It is this ongoing process of risking and experimenting, of failing and being encouraged, of blessing and risking again that creates the environment for real missional transformation when we are in the clearing.

5. Commitment

As people internalize this way of life, they begin to understand the framework of transformation. The ordinary men and women of a local church now begin to actively innovate mission-shaped life across the church because they have listened to each other; they have been given the dignity of God's people, and they have discovered that the Spirit of God really is present among them. It is at this point, in the midst of growing experiments, that people realize that they have discovered for themselves a way of being church that isn't dependent on outside programs, gurus, or even ordained clergy. Tangible, measurable, and observable actions occur. This is the point at which a local church tips over to a place from which it can't go back to the old ways of being passive recipients of religious goods and services.

The following chapters provide details about how a church moves through the Missional Change Model. By necessity our description in these chapters views the process from about twenty thousand feet.

In other words, we can't give you all the nitty-gritty details here. You can find more details, tools, and coaching processes at www .roxburghmissionalnet.com, along with the *Mission-Shaped Church Field Guide*, which serves as a workbook for specific churches to work through the details of the Missional Change Model.

This is the basic outline of the elements in the Missional Change Model. As we said in introducing the model, it isn't a linear process, as if once we have gone through the steps we are done. Far from it! As people learn the language of the model and begin testing it for themselves, they will spiral back and forth across the various steps so that soon there is nothing linear about it at all. This is what makes the model so powerful and creative. It's not a box we fit people into but a way of learning together how to travel into places we have never been before. It allows people to be in different places at different times and yet still create a culture of experimentation and innovation from among the people rather than from the top down.

11

The Awareness Stage

Staring Reality in the Face

A woman expresses her confusion when she laments that her two sons no longer go to church and now she is watching her grandchildren grow up without any Christian formation. A young couple who once served on the staff of a Christian youth organization confess they have stopped attending any church because what's happening inside the church now is out of touch with the realities of life that young people face. A church board looks at statistics for the previous year and wonders why its best efforts to improve the church's future have not amounted to any effective growth. A pastor in his forties has worked incalculable hours to grow a church in a new suburban neighborhood, but lately he is quietly asking himself if he wants to spend the rest of his life creating amazing programs and Sunday events for people transferring in from other churches.

This is just a small sample of some of the stories we have heard, and we are sure you could also tell stories about what people are facing who find themselves in this clearing. It is a new place with concrete and personal realities that go way beyond church statistics and common trends about belief patterns in America, which are often the focus of books and seminars that tell pastors how to be the church. In this new clearing people feel the crisis; they want to know what has happened to their churches and why things don't work like they once did.

One of the first steps of the missional journey is taken when we open our eyes to the many ways people in our local churches and their neighborhoods feel and experience this clearing. This involves turning attention away from a preoccupation with our need to achieve or change something and attend to what is happening in our people. The most basic step happens in any number of ways, but it involves creating safe spaces where people believe they are being listened to and in which they are able to give voice to their experiences in this clearing.

Where Is There Space?

Within the local church, people know they now live in a time of immense change. They are confused by these changes and conflicted about what to do with it all because what they see and feel going on is so deep and disturbing that it cuts to their very hearts. Here are some more stories:

- A couple sits in a small group describing the conversation they have just had with their daughter, who is home from college. It always had been their conviction that their church was working well and that their children found a place in it for themselves. But their daughter told them she just can't connect anymore with her parents' church.
- An architect who just turned sixty wonders why he is so dissatisfied with the renewal church in which he has invested twenty years of his life. The songs and the sermons just don't seem to connect with the world with which his adult children are wrestling.
- A young entrepreneur drives his family to the big, regional church multiple times each week. It feels like they have developed a taxi service for church programs. Recently he has been asked to serve on the board, but he realizes that he has no time to be in his neighborhood because he's so busy doing church

148

work. He wonders, "Is this really what it means to serve in the kingdom and follow Jesus?"

- A businesswoman leaves for work at 6:30 a.m. and returns at 7:00 p.m. with little time for her family. Weekends are spent on housework and shopping. At work she's responsible for more than 1,500 employees, many of whom are about to lose their jobs due to outsourcing overseas. She wonders about the church she has long known. How does she make sense of being a Christian in the midst of all this?

- A middle-aged couple watches people from faraway countries with strange religious practices move into their neighborhood. Some of these people are quite hospitable. They seem to have strong families that celebrate their togetherness, their moral lives seem impeccable, and their quality of life seems quite high even though they don't have many of the possessions a good income brings. In church the couple is told that Jesus is the only way to God, but they are struggling with what the Christian faith means in this new kind of world.

- High school students deal with feelings of abandonment as their middle-class parents work long hours in an attempt to make ends meet. At church youth group they only go through the motions because they don't know how to talk about their impression that all the programs fail to address what is really going on in their lives.

Where do we give space in our churches for people to talk about these realities? How do we create environments for people to share their frustrations? It is hard to find a person in church today who is not thinking, feeling, or talking about these kinds of issues. And if we don't give room in the church for people to share how they view life, they will just talk elsewhere, and most of the time such talk will become unhealthy. These people don't just feel alone with their questions and feelings; most of them also don't have any safe places to express their confusion and freely admit their inability to make sense of the world that surrounds them. Therefore the first step to the development of a mission-shaped church is to give voice to what is happening among the people. Following are some ways this can be done.

Pastoral Care

Classic pastoral care is a key way to give people voice. Pastoral care at its best is about asking the question, "How is your soul?" As any seasoned leader knows, one doesn't start with this question but works at creating safe spaces where the question can be asked. This might involve connecting with people on a regular basis without an agenda, asking questions that are genuinely open-ended, and inviting people to share something of what is happening in their lives. This is how church leaders can genuinely begin to create an environment in which people feel listened into free speech.

Our experience is that other people rarely ask us about our lives at a deeper level than, "Hi, how are you?" unless they want something from us. What would it be like to cultivate a church in which people ask deeper questions without strings attached? What is important to emphasize is that we don't need to have answers in order to create this space for people. In fact, having all the answers and Bible verses on hand runs contrary to what we are trying to do. We need an environment in which people feel safe to give voice to what is happening inside them right now.

Appreciative Inquiry

Another way we go about creating this environment is through the use of questions. A friend of ours, Mark Lau Branson, who teaches at Fuller Seminary, has written a wonderful little book called *Memories, Hopes and Conversations: Appreciative Inquiry and Congregational Change*.[1] He documents how this process of listening people into free speech can happen in a church that has closed in on itself and no longer experiences the safety to speak about what is actually happening among the people. Branson's book then provides directions that can be used to develop this sort of listening process in a local church. The questions he suggests are not programmatic tactics for getting people to do something in the church; they simply offer a way to listen to one another. The conviction that shapes Branson's book is that in and among the stories of the people of a church are all the clues for discerning the dreams and ways of life the Spirit is calling forth for that people in that place.

Giving Language to People's Experiences

One of the ways we invite people into conversation about what is happening to them is through a simple set of workshops that can be offered over a weekend or as a learning series over a number of weeks. These workshops, or conversation events, are designed to assist people in finding new language for what they are experiencing in the clearing. The workshop we use, called Surfing the Edge,[2] uses the metaphor of maps to invite people into dialogue about the changes they are experiencing. Instead of giving people answers, we have designed a process in which the people themselves work at identifying these changes and talking about why they have become so difficult to manage.

The workshop then goes on to talk about the Scripture stories of people who meet God in places of massive change (desert, exile, wilderness, and so on) and how these are the places where God always does something wonderfully new among them. Finally, we talk about the ways of listening to one another's stories, creating dialogue, and learning again to listen to Scripture as key ways of becoming God's missionary people in our neighborhoods. In our experience this kind of event (or series of evening events in the local church) goes a long way toward preparing and inviting people into a journey of missional transformation.

Forming Listening Teams

The primary way we facilitate awareness in local churches is by forming a team of people from within the church who will carry out a series of listening conversations across the church over a three- to four-month period. We make sure the team is comprised of people who are not on the staff or board so that it is clear from the start that this is a process of ordinary people listening to and learning from one another rather than a new program designed by the staff for the church. In other words, the listening process must be primarily a bottom-up or, to use a terrible word, lay-driven process. We train this team in some simple steps for doing these listening interviews. It is always interesting to see the level of anxiety people bring with them into this process. Even very talented people who run effective organizations outside their church need to ask a lot of questions to make sure they are getting the process right. What we have discovered after doing this for a number of years is that many people no longer find their local church a safe place to talk.

The listening team members will conduct a series of interviews with people in the church over several months using a common set of questions to ask in each interview. Over time about sixty interviews are conducted, depending on the size of the church. At each interview the team member takes notes about the ways people respond. Following is an example of the kinds of questions we use. Although these are not all the questions nor are they complete, they give you a taste of what happens.

For more information on this process see the Mission-Shaped Church Field Guide

1. Reflect back on your entire experience at our church. When did you feel most engaged, alive, and motivated? What was happening that contributed to that experience?
2. What do you think are the most important, life-giving characteristics of our church?
3. When are we at our best?
4. Describe a time in our church when God was most real and alive for you.

all A-I. questions!

These interviews are designed to set the stage, cultivate the soil, and create an environment in which people come to believe that what they have to say is important and that their stories help identify who they are as a local church. And the kinds of stories that are told will be amazing. They are often stories, lost or forgotten, about the ways in which God's Spirit has been at work, moving among his people in wonderful ways. The questions help people discover that God is still up to something in their church and that we find God's future as we reenter the stories of the people.

Team members also ask people to identify issues they see others wrestling with now. In order to receive real answers, the interviewers have to build trust and communicate that they want to listen to them and hear God through them. This takes time.

Our experience has revealed that this is a crucial beginning point. When we have asked the listening team to reflect on their own experiences in doing the interviews, they report that people were amazed that they were asked. Some people responded, "Do you really care about what I think?" Others asked, "Can I be honest?" One man, almost in tears, said, "I've been in this church for almost ten years and no one has ever asked me what I thought about things."

Listening team members say things like: "We are learning how to listen to one another as a church in ways we don't seem to have done for a very long time." What is always interesting about these interviews is that when people are asked to participate, they automatically assume something is wrong. They are amazed and wonderfully surprised to discover that nothing is wrong but that we want to learn how to listen to the Spirit through one another.

From these interviews a listening report is developed, and what we do with it is very important. We don't use them to create an analysis of the church and its people; we do everything possible to stay away from an expert or abstract analysis. Several things happen to the reports, and we tell people ahead of time how they will be used. First, we gather a new team of people from across the church—including some from the original listening team, but also inviting others new to the process (again making sure that no church staff are on the team). These people read all the interview reports, looking at them with these kinds of questions in mind:

- Are there any themes that keep coming up in these reports?
- What images and metaphors are present in people's responses?
- What might be missing or not talked about in the interviews?
- Where is God seen in these responses, and how is he seen to be active or inactive?
- What are the signs of hope?

The group's task, then, is not to write an analysis of what they are reading but to identify the key questions that are raised by the reports. At the same time, the listening report is given to a small group of people from outside the church. These are generally people who know something of the tradition of this local church and are good at reading with listening hearts. They ask the same set of questions as the internal team. We then gather the two sets of responses to create a comprehensive report that is comprised of a brief overview of the listening interview responses.

What we are doing in this process is creating an environment of listening that lets everyone know their stories and imagination are key to the Spirit's work. Rather than presenting people with an expert analysis, the comprehensive report provides additional questions that help people continue the conversations and move deeper into the process of listening to one another. The next chapter explains how we do that.

Before we finish this chapter, however, it is important to emphasize that this is a process of dialogue. Developing awareness is about beginning to create an environment in which people believe that their voices have a place in God's purposes. It is a gradual process—awareness is not a time slot to move through in order to get to the next stage. We are in the process of cultivating a way of life as a local church rather than moving through a program. This first stage might take four to eight months to initiate—the amount of time doesn't matter. Once begun, it is something that becomes a part of the rhythm, the warp and woof of the church's life. If this doesn't happen, people will know that the processes of listening and dialogue were nothing more than another method of getting them to do something, and that will shut down any attempt at cultivating a missionary people.

Timeline at a Glance

This new awareness begins a process of entering into the Missional Change Model introduced in the previous chapter. The following chapters present an initial guide for the journey beyond awareness and offer an explanation of the *why* and *what* of each step to provide you with a basis for understanding how to go about the process of missional change in your local church.

Table 3

Missional Change Timeline

Chapter	Stage	Time	Description
11	Deciding	3–6 months prior	Workshops: What Is Missional Church?
	Awareness	Months 1–2	Listening teams Listening team report
12	Understanding	Months 3–5	Mission-shaped church questionnaire Feedback seminar
13	Evaluating	Months 6–8	Dialogue groups Naming missional challenges Board/leaders identify primary challenges and teams
15	Experimenting	Months 9–14	Missional action groups "Practicing Hospitality" small groups
Conclusion	Commitment	Month 15	Action team reports Hospitality reports
		Month 16	Initiate new missional experiments
		Months 17–18	Next steps

The experience of giving voice to what we are going through in the clearing is very personal. None of us like to admit that we find ourselves in a place where we can no longer adequately give words to what is happening. We are reluctant to own how this is affecting and disturbing us; we need words that will give our experiences some meaning in this new place. This is akin to a mountain climber looking for grips in the rock face in which to place his or her hands and feet. These grips aren't like neatly arranged stairs we can easily walk up without effort. They are more like small outcroppings that help us get a grip and find ways of moving farther up the mountain. Awareness is like finding these toeholds in order to take the next steps. Now that we have these toeholds, on to the next stage.

12

The Understanding Stage

Can We Really Talk about These Things?

The Missional Change Model envisions a movement that begins with awareness and moves toward understanding. In the awareness stage we invite each other to find the language that makes sense of our own internal experiences and feelings of being in the clearing. The understanding stage begins as people tentatively find this language and are therefore able to talk to one another about their experiences. In one sense, then, awareness is a more personal, internal process of finding that *aha* place where I am able to give words to my experiences, while understanding is when I begin to test this awareness in *dialogue* with others. This dialogue deepens our understanding of what is happening to us in the clearing.

It is important to remember that this process is about transforming how we go about being a missional community of God's people. It is about a corporate, communal transformation. While it necessarily involves personal work and takes seriously the conviction that each person we are working and partnering with can never be turned into an object of some plan or missional goals, we must keep before us this focus on a corporate process of missional transformation. In the clearing we are being formed as the people of God, not simply

157

individuals using God for some process of self-development in the midst of trying times.

The Listening Report

The listening report that resulted from the initial round of conversations helps us to deepen awareness and enter the understanding stage. It is a prelude to inviting everyone to join in conversation centered around the report. Again, this is a very gentle, simple process. We are communicating through some of the questions we asked and the stories we have heard that God has been part of the church for a long time; we are lifting up the hope of people as they hear again the stories of God's faithfulness. By raising open-ended questions from the listening report, we are inviting people to continue the dialogue rather than closing it down with conclusions.

All of this builds trust for people to continue to risk giving voice to their own experience in the church. The venues for these ongoing conversations can be varied. Small groups might take a few weeks to talk about the report and engage some of the questions it brings up. Sunday programs, such as classes or discussion groups, can interact with the questions as they move a little deeper into a dialogue of awareness and understanding. Each time a group meets to discuss the questions, someone should keep a record of what is said. These one or two pages of notes are then given to what we call a *guiding team* that provides oversight for the overall process. All of this builds interest and trust; it creates a buzz among people and in so doing cultivates a readiness for the next step.

The Mission-Shaped Church 360

Some years ago Alan was given a digital camera for Christmas. After all the Christmas Day festivities, he managed to get the entire family—children, spouses, baby grandchildren, and dogs (four of them at the time)—captured in pictures. He immediately went into his office, downloaded the pictures onto the computer, and printed off a bunch of copies.

As copies of Alan's freshly printed photograph were passed around the living room, an amazing conversation began. Stories started to come out. At first it was humorous and fun. Sara Jane took the picture and said, "Look at Mom; she is always gathering us together, bringing us into a group like this." It was a loving poke at Jane and a confession of great appreciation and love for a mother who made the family the center of all our lives. The conversations continued. Someone remarked how different so-and-so looked in the photograph compared to just a few years earlier. Everyone knew what that meant, smiling with relief and thanksgiving for the changes God works in our lives. It was a wonderful conversation stimulated by a digital photograph of the family together.

As Alan reflected on this experience, a new set of questions developed: What might it look like if we could take something like a photograph of a local church? What if we could take a group shot at a moment in time and then invite people to talk with each other about the picture? Would this assist us in cultivating the kind of dialogue that creates a safe space for listening one another into free speech? How might this be done? From these questions, he and his friend Fred Romanuk began to design a questionnaire. If we could get a high percentage of a local church to participate, we could produce a kind of composite snapshot of the church and then invite people to talk together about what they see.

The work produced the Mission-Shaped 360, and it became the primary tool we use for developing understanding in the Mission Change Model. It is called a 360 because it invites everyone in the church—like a full circle—to contribute to the conversation about how the church might go on mission in its community. It does this through a series of steps: (1) Everyone is invited to complete the online questionnaire. (2) On the basis of all the responses, a feedback report is created. The report is like a photograph reflecting back to the church the ways differing groups read its readiness for missional transformation. (3) The report becomes the basis for inviting everyone into a series of conversations concerning what the Spirit might be saying about some potential missional experiments in the neighborhoods and communities of the people. These three steps are explained in more detail below.

159

1. Complete the Online 360

The first step is for people to complete the online 360. Central to the effectiveness of the 360 is to get as many people as possible in the church to complete it. If you want a churchwide photograph, you should do it during a time when the most people are involved in church life so you don't leave anyone out. Invite everyone to contribute to this point-in-time photograph, which in turn will create more ownership in the process. Those who cannot use computers or may be intimidated by an online questionnaire can fill out a hard copy, and then volunteers transfer their responses into an online format.

> The Mission-Shaped 360 can be accessed at www.roxburghmissional net.com along with additional information regarding how the 360 and the report work.

Remember, the idea here is that you are seeking to achieve a deepening awareness and understanding by creating environments of dialogue around listening to the Spirit through one another. The 360 assists you in this and helps you find out who you are as a local church right now and what the Spirit might be saying to you. It is a journey in trusting the Spirit in the midst of your people.

2. Feedback Report

All of the data from the completed 360s is compiled and processed to produce a report, which is the photograph of the church. There are many layers and perspectives that this report provides. It begins with a very broad view of the data, which is like looking at the entire picture from the perspective of 50,000 feet above the earth. Then it moves through greater and greater specificity until each of the various questions is analyzed.

One thing that must be recognized about this report is that it is quite different from other churchwide 360s, such as church health assessments or best practices measurements. This is *not* a prescriptive report that tells you what needs to be done to become a missional church. Nor does it compare your church with some other group of churches. This difference must be clear in the minds of the people. In fact, we are convinced that measuring and comparing one church with another shuts down the essential dialogue needed to cultivate a missional imagination in a local church. The purpose of the 360 is to generate dialogue and interaction among the people themselves.

Some people are initially concerned that this kind of report might create conflict if people talk about their different understandings. Actually, the opposite is true. We have used this resource in hundreds of local churches, always with the same result: as people engage with the feedback report, they become energized because they are finally able to talk to one another, to tell stories about how they are seeing things, and to be heard. In one case we introduced this report to a large church that was facing conflict and was concerned that its leadership staff wasn't listening to the people. By the end of the day the group was engaged with one another, laughing at the reality they saw, and energized because they could really talk to one another about their church and its hope for missional life.

3. Feedback Seminar

Once the report is assembled, a date is set for a feedback seminar. This one-day event, or several evenings close together, does two basic things: (1) It helps people understand the report and interpret it for themselves so they can understand that it's not a measurement or comparison but a *photograph* inviting dialogue. (2) The next steps are introduced. This involves committing three to four months in dialogue groups, talking together about elements of the report and asking the question, "On the basis of these conversations, what experiments in missional life might the Spirit be calling us to in our neighborhoods and communities?" The next chapter introduces this stage of the missional transformation process.

13

The Evaluation Stage

A Snapshot of the Church

The report received by the church is a specific type of photograph taken at a particular moment in time. When a family goes to the photographer, the desire is for a family portrait that will be framed and hung on the wall for posterity. The photograph in the report is far more informal. It is a series of snapshots of groups of people. Imagine it more in terms of a summer party where lots of people are swirling around in conversation groups all over the house. You grab the digital camera and move about from one conversation group to the next snapping unposed moments in the midst of the party. This is what the report is like. As we assemble the different snapshots, we are creating a summary of how differing groups across a local church perceive the readiness of the church to engage in missional change. Now what is to be done with these snapshots?

People will want to talk together about the report, and they will need time and a structure that allows them to do so. This is the evaluation stage, which is about asking how the newfound awareness and understanding speak into the current practices of the church. People are invited into a dialogue process to evaluate how their church practices relate to its call to be mission-shaped people in the neighborhoods where they live. In this phase we talk together about our readiness as a church to be on mission and discern some potential ways we might do that. We recommend a four-month process of dialogue groups in which the feedback report is processed together.

Don't Short-Circuit the Journey

This is a stage when leaders are tempted to shorten the process by moving too quickly to action plans and strategies. We must resist this temptation and allow people to develop an understanding that the answers to their lives as God's mission-shaped people are among *them*, not in the hands of experts and professionals (i.e., reverends, pastors, and people with doctorates and master's degrees). In most church traditions the people have been shaped by a culture of experts and professionals to such an extent that they assume the sources of direction and the answers to the challenges they need to address lie outside themselves in paid staff, hired consultants, and purchased programs. As we have stated before, the understanding of missional transformation presented in this book operates on a set of very different convictions, and the default of abdicating to professionals and experts is so strong in church culture that this point bears repeating. We must not short-circuit the journey at this point. We must allow understanding to rise from the bottom up and resist the temptation to provide easy answers. Just in case you are not yet convinced of this perspective, we will give a summary of why these dialogue groups are so crucial to the journey at this point.   *? or dig continuous*

We find ourselves in a place of massive, continuous change. We have entered a clearing where none of us have been before, and our maps no longer describe the landscape in front of us. In this new place experts and professionals are of little assistance. They are like the Israelites in Egypt who were forced to make bricks. These great brick makers became the leaders of the community; their experience and wisdom guided the people in tough times. But in the desert, brick makers were no longer the experts—you can't make bricks in a desert. The temptation in this clearing is to want to find a way of going back to the time and place where things worked for us. We gradually learn that there is really no going back.

Another temptation in this clearing is to find a guru who promises us that he or she has discovered the way, ancient or new, and is now ready to guide us like the Pied Piper of another time. Many will follow, but most will discover that it's a dangerous thing to trust gurus with their visions of what we need to be. The biblical narratives tell us over and over again that this clearing (usually called "desert" or "exile" in the biblical narratives) is not a place to escape from but the place where God does something outrageously imaginative and transformative. Therefore we are called to live in this unsettling place and carry on with a lot of the normal things we have been doing rather than trying to reorganize. It is in this place that we discover some of the most fantastic things about the ways of God.

The Spirit of God is among the people of God, not in the experts and the ordained, but right in the midst of all the ordinary men and women of the local church. This means that God's very Spirit is in the local church, among the ordinary men, women, and children who comprise this faith community. Therefore God's imagination and God's future is among these ordinary local men and women who gather to worship, who confess their confusion, who know the church is messed up and needs to change, and who confess that they don't have a clue what might be involved in this change or how to go about it. This is where the Spirit is at work. How dare anyone write off the church! This means that the answer to the question, "What is God calling us to be in the communities where we live and work?" is among the people, not in experts or outside consultants or even in some program that worked somewhere else. And therefore, the job of the leadership is not to come up with grand plans for the congregation but to cultivate an environment in which the missional imagination of the people of God is called forth in lived action and lives. This happens as we create spaces and time for people to trust their own voice as a people, to dwell together in the Word, to listen one another into free speech, and to dare to ask in dialogue with one another what the Spirit might want them to risk in connecting with their neighborhoods and communities.

This is why we use the feedback report to initiate a three- to four-month period when people meet in groups to listen to the Spirit. It is about discernment and about the dignity of the people of God.

What Is Dialogue?

Dialogue is like setting a wonderful table covered with a delight-
ful assortment of food to which we welcome others to join. Often
when people are invited to a meal, they wonder what the host wants
from them. They become suspicious that the host has an agenda or
that there is something he or she wants to sell us; so the guests go
cautiously, with reservation. It's nice to be invited, but they wonder
what it's really about.

So when we invite people for a meal, we need to recognize this
dynamic might be present and therefore seek to create a table that
sets them at ease. This can be done by asking questions of genuine
interest and asking them about themselves. To genuinely build relationships of trust in which others will become ready to risk and
talk with us about who they are, what they think, and their tentative
dreams that have long been locked away inside, we need to sit around
a meal table on more than one occasion until the others begin to sense
that they are not the subject of our agenda. This is what dialogue is
about: it is the context in which the freedom and imagination of the
Holy Spirit have the potential of coming to speak among ordinary
people who have long believed they cannot possibly be the clay jars
that bear God's future.

Without a venue for dialogue, a local church won't enter into this
delicate, tender place of listening, dialogue, and missional discernment. That is why rushing to design tactics and strategies at this point
is like forcing a plant to blossom before it is ready. This dialogue
around the report takes time, and time is what we have, because in
Christ's church people are never objects to be used—they are vessels
of the Spirit's imagination for mission. The 360 report is a tool that
invites the congregation to step back from plans and solutions and
take a rare opportunity to talk with one another about what they
are observing in the rich responses of the report.

When this occurs, groups begin to see what is below the surface.
Figure 14 illustrates why this is the case.

The image is somewhat out of proportion, but it illustrates a point.
We are used to seeing a tree in terms of what is aboveground—the
trunk, branches, and leaves. We know that under the surface are root

Figure 14

The Rules of Dialogue

1. Explain the nature of dialogue and lay out expectations from the beginning. Make sure everyone knows that the 360 was designed to ensure that there are no right or wrong answers or positions.
2. The first three responses to one another should come in the form of questions for clarification rather than giving reasons why someone's comments or ideas are wrong or won't work.
3. The group must strive to create an environment in which everyone knows they are being heard and understood.
4. Listen to the others by letting them finish what they are saying rather than jumping into the middle of their comments. Stay away from remarks like, "I disagree." For most people this will shut down their contributions.
5. Resist announcing conclusions or solutions that try to fix things. Instead work together at keeping the conversations open.

systems, but we tend to take those for granted, giving attention to what stands before us in the form of the tree.

What we want to do in the dialogue groups is get beneath the surface by continuing to dialogue with one another about what we think might be going on in the root system. We do not do this by asking an expert to come in and give us an analysis of how he or she sees things; we do it by continuing the process of awareness and understanding. This is why listening to one another is so important. So much of what actually shapes and drives what we do as local churches is in the *roots*, but we pay most of our attention to the *trunks*, *branches*, and *leaves*. In fact, most planning in churches is based on what we see aboveground. So this is an opportunity to look at the roots as we listen more deeply to one another.

Forming the Dialogue Groups

Many churches structure themselves around some type of small group program. This ranges from informal Bible study or encouragement groups on up to staffed, small group programs that function as the primary relational and discipleship structure of the church. Some churches even define themselves as a church of small groups. Small groups, at their best, are an amazing tool; they are an organic, natural way in which people form community and get things done.

In this stage it is essential to form dialogue groups that are different from established small groups in order to develop communication across some entrenched boundaries; we want groups in which people are dialoguing with folks from different circles. Missional transformation is about boundary crossing and learning to be with others and listen them into free speech. If we can't do that with the others in our local churches—the persons who sit in other pews or whom we pass in the vestibule—how will we ever learn to welcome and listen into free speech the stranger across the street or colleagues at work? Groups must cross generations, ethnicity, gender, and geography so that we create as diverse a table as possible. We do this by making it clear why these groups are meeting, the nature of their task, and the limited time period they will meet. All of this lowers anxiety and provides safety for people to risk participation. When people are assured through clear communication that they will be able to return to their usual small group, they are more likely to choose to participate in a process that might seem unclear with end results that are still unknown.

The dialogue groups should be comprised of five to seven people. Each group will meet about once every three weeks over a three-month period. The dialogue groups receive a package that contains a selected group of pages from the feedback report. A recorder will keep notes of the conversations as people interact with the report pages and the supplied questions. This is the rhythm shaping the first three of the four group meetings.

The fourth, or final, group meeting gathers the previous conversations to ask the question: What does all this mean for who we are as a church at this point in time in terms of God's calling for us to be a mission-shaped people in our neighborhoods and communities? As simple as this question may sound or as easy as it is to write on a page, it is a very difficult question to answer. There are going to be a variety of responses from the group, and most of them will be unspoken, even in a context that has sought to create spaces of welcome and safety. But these unspoken responses will control what happens in the room if they are not addressed.

What might be some of those responses? A few in the room may have waited a long time for this opportunity to state what they absolutely believe the church must do to be faithful in witness. When they state it with conviction, it may sound to others in the room that all this process around missional transformation is going to mean a radical change of everything that the church has done to this point, a restructuring of its life, a set of disruptive changes. For many this could create fear and the kind of anxiety that causes some to react and shut down the conversation. Others might feel that decisions are starting to be made that do not have the approval of the staff or official board. To address these potential killers of the process, it is important to provide people with guidelines for this fourth and crucial group meeting. Many of the details of these guidelines are discussed in the next chapters as we describe the work of the church board and the nature of the experiments that will be created. Briefly, the guidelines we give the group are as follows:

In this final meeting we want to gather together our previous conversations and begin to ask, tentatively, what God may be saying to us about some potential ways we, as a church, might try a few experiments in missional life in our neighborhoods and communities. We are not trying to say we know for sure exactly what the Spirit is saying to us, but we believe the Spirit of God is among us as a church and together we can learn to test what the Spirit might be saying. All we are looking for are simple, potential experiments in mission in our neighborhoods and communities. Right now we are not looking to change programs or structures or roles in the church. That may come in the future, but for now we just want to listen to what the Spirit might be saying. What we will do is record our responses, and then we will take our responses and those of all the other dialogue groups and give them to the church board. They will then meet together on a retreat and, in prayer together, they as our spiritual leaders will consider all these responses and seek to discern the two or three experiments they believe the Spirit is calling us as a church to begin with.

By framing the meeting in this way, we create a context of safety that addresses most people's potential anxieties. We take from people what might be the burden of *getting it right*, and we free them to ask what might be the calling of the Spirit. By framing it in the language of *experiments*, we take away the anxiety of those who think this may mean a lot of change. We will talk more about experiments and board work in the following chapters.

14

The Work of the Church Board

How Do Innovators and Traditionalists
Work Together?

When the dialogue groups have completed their process, the board and leadership of the congregation assemble all the reports, which are then used by the board to guide its own discernment process as the board members identify several specific *challenges* or *experiments* from the suggestions of the dialogue groups. The board members are the ones who lead the church in the process of spiritual discernment, so they should be a primary group in the process of missional transformation. But they also need safety, space, and time to see and learn how to do this. The process we outline in this chapter is designed to achieve these goals.

The Work of the Church Board

Across most church systems the church board members (session, board, elders, vestry, or deacons, depending on the ecclesiology of the system) are called to provide spiritual oversight of the church. The basic question they seek to address is: What are the purposes and directions of God for this community of believers within our church traditions? Of course we recognize that this description is often more the ideal than the reality. Too often church boards become little more than the business unit of the church or those who feel they must ensure that everything is done according to the by-laws and constitution.

Our purpose here is neither to be naive in assuming most boards function out of a basic spiritual discernment stance nor to neglect the fact that this is one of their primary roles in their church. Across all traditions is this basic recognition that these kinds of boards are responsible for discerning the directions of God among the people. This doesn't mean they should act like CEOs or that they have the right to huddle and come up with some kind of mission, vision, or preferred-future plan for the church. They are called to listen to the Spirit at work in the church and guide the local body into the way of mission.

In most cases those who are elected to a church board are ones who are respected by the community because of their character and established patterns of life. They have been around, and they are trusted. This trust is usually based on an assessment that they understand the traditions of the church. In other words, the board members are the holders of the memory of the past and the established habits of the community. This means they will tend to see their roles in terms of conserving and maintaining. This is appropriate since the ability to live in and appreciate the continuing tradition (the narratives) of the people is a critical gift in terms of any community's continuity and ability to thrive.

Furthermore, the type of person elected to a board is usually someone with the ability to manage the church on the basis of the past. This means the orientation of board members is more to the question, "What are the well-established ways of doing things?" rather than, "What are the fresh expressions of mission and ministry we need to develop?" This is not a criticism of the people on a board; it is only an attempt to realistically assess the current status of most boards. These are gifted people with a certain way of approaching their responsibilities.

In the first place, it is usually the church leadership who first get involved in the missional change process. This happens in a number of ways. In our experience, for example, a cluster of local churches in a denominational region are invited to consider being part of the process by the executive of the region. When this happens there is usually a period of five to six months when church board members have a chance to talk about the process and how it will work. These are initial conversations in which the board members start to get a feel for what might be involved, but they aren't going to understand it all initially. Remember, we are inviting people to take a journey into a space they have never been before. It's not possible to grasp the whole process at the front door. Sometimes people ask us for a map that outlines the whole process, such as the one provided at the beginning of chapter 10 along with a timeline of the steps. These resources help the board start to get the picture, but in order to move into a missional transformation, it is only really going to be learned and discovered along the way.

Next, because this is a process of learning as we go along, we do several things to assure the board members that they are a vital part of the process and that nothing will change without their discussion and permission. This is why we take the time to tell them that in this process we are not working on organizational, structural, program, or role change. This lowers their anxiety. At that point we speak in terms of experiments and show the board members how they will always be involved in the process and receive regular communication about the nature of these experiments. Then we invite the board to identify a team who will guide the process in the church while keeping them informed. This leaves the board free to do its important, ongoing work. As we will see, it also gives the board its own safe space to watch the process unfold, because we make it clear that board members can be involved at all levels of the process even though they are not to take the lead on managing and shaping it in the church. In this way the board can learn for itself without needing to take massive risks with a process they are only starting to learn.

How the Missional Journey Should Be Overseen

Most of the board members we have encountered are aware of the need for significant change in the life of the church, but they have little experience with leading this kind of transformation. As a result they tend to champion projects that focus on small improvements of what they are already doing. Furthermore, when people are elected to boards they feel the responsibility of doing a good job. Even if they sense the church is struggling or even declining, they feel a duty to be cautious and not do anything that might negatively impact the church. They don't want to make mistakes, so the more they sense the vulnerability or fragility of the church, the more cautious they become.

In the context of these realities, the board must have the authority to determine the experiments with which the local church will begin, but board members will not actually have to participate in the experiments unless they feel called to do so. They will identify a group (or several groups) of people in the church who will initiate experiments, and then this group will meet with them at specific times along the way to update them about what the group is doing. In this way the board feels ownership for what is happening, and they can learn, get inside, and evaluate the process of experimenting and its relationship to mission-shaped transformation.

What follows is an outline of the board's role and relationship to the missional transformation process. The purpose of the first three phases has been to achieve four goals:

1. Initiate a congregation-wide process of dialogue that develops awareness and understanding of the board's own readiness to engage in mission within its geographic community and the neighborhoods where the church members live.
2. Identify several key missional ways the church might create experiments in missional formation.
3. Assist the church and its leaders to understand the nature of experiments rather than reinforce more attractional programs that have shaped their lives in the past.
4. Gain trust and commitment to an ongoing process of missional experiments.

The board plays a key role in all of this in a number of ways. For instance, unless the board enters the processes, it is impossible to diffuse missional change through the church so that it becomes an

174

essential part of its life. In addition, the board has a very powerful ability to veto, whether passively or actively, and must sense that it is engaged with the process at every stage. This does not mean the board must lead and invest a lot of its time in the process, but it must have a sense that it understands the reasons for the process as well as the steps involved.

In order to do this, some basic understanding of the Missional Change Model is necessary. All of this work can be done in partnership with church staff as the early listening processes are occurring. When introduced in this way as a part of the board's learning and discernment work, board members can take time to read, learn, and talk together about these concepts. The pastoral staff can lead workshops in these processes as well as meet with board members in smaller groups in which they can talk more openly about what they are learning and how they are responding to these new ideas. At the same time, it is important to continually emphasize that this transformation process is not about changing structures or roles but discovering Spirit-guided experiments in mission-shaped life. This assurance, in the midst of learning about transformation, lowers the anxiety and heightens the ability to learn new ideas.

Preparing the Board to Oversee the Journey

There are multiple ways to provide the necessary information for board members to attain an understanding and to feel comfortable about the missional change process. We will discuss three of them here.

1. Hold a Workshop

A number of boards from several churches could gather together for a workshop on "What Is Missional Church?"[1] This might be divided over several months of board meetings or be presented as a whole in one board retreat. This creates a safe space for board members to collaborate, learn, and ask questions.

In sharing the vision of the missional church, it is crucial that the board members have time and space to process what they are learning. The issues and questions that arise from these conversations will provide clues about the additional information that will be required. When introducing a new idea, we must recognize that most people need to go back over the same information ten to fifteen times before they understand what is being said, so do not rely on a one-time event or informational meeting to achieve the necessary communication. This means that a dialogue process using various methods of communication is very important. One way to initiate this dialogue is through a trusted member of the wider system's staff (e.g., synod, presbytery, conference, association) who knows the history and traditions of the church and can speak out of this knowledge into the realities of the church. This can help gain the trust of the board members.

At the workshop, create group times when board members can process together what they are learning and thinking. During this time, listen to their questions and issues, because they provide important clues as to where the board members are in the process as well as the points at which they will require further dialogue and engagement. Staff members may want to provide a series of questions for board members to discuss, which will significantly increase the learning.

2. Explain the Entire Process

It is important to walk the board members through the steps that will be involved for the church. Give them lots of space to ask their questions, and be patient in terms of the time they will need to feel comfortable. Introduce them to and make sure each of them has a copy of the *Mission-Shaped Church Field Guide*[2] so that they can see the steps and feel they have a reference point from which to respond when others ask them questions. Engage the board with the rationale for the questionnaire and explain the process of working through the feedback report.

3. Gather at a Retreat

The board must receive and discuss the feedback report before it goes to the whole church. This gives the board the security and information it needs to move forward in an adaptive process. Board ownership develops as they evaluate the listening responses and identify the challenges they believe the congregation must address. As pointed out earlier, once all the listening group reports are completed, the next critical role of the board is to evaluate the feedback from the congregation and then discern the appropriate experiments to initiate. A recommended method for doing this is during an overnight retreat (Friday evening through Saturday afternoon).[3]

At this retreat the board chooses the experiments, reviews how the experiments will work, and identifies people who might form the experiment team. The idea is that several easy-win experiments will be initiated and carried out while keeping in dialogue with the board. In this way the board, as well as the rest of the church, begin to see that these experiments are not threatening and do not undercut the life of the church. This enables both the board and the church members to start imagining other potential experiments they might want to initiate. This experiment process will be described in the next chapter.

How the Board Works with the Missional Experiment Team

We have a carefully developed process that enables the board to both learn and stay in touch with these experiments. At the retreat where the board chooses the initial challenges, we also assist them to identify the people in the church whom they want to initiate these experiments. These are usually people who are the early adopters, are ready for a challenge, and are eager to move forward into new ventures. After identifying these people, the board gives them their mandate. The following is a map of how we do this in a local congregation. There are many other ways to go about it, but what we are seeking to achieve here is for the board members to learn in their own time how the experiment process works while not being asked to risk the experiment themselves. Instead they are invited to dialogue with the team as it works on some of the first sets of experiments. This enables board members to get inside the process and own it for themselves.

The stages are quite straightforward.[4]

- The board gives the team the challenge or experiment they have chosen at the retreat.

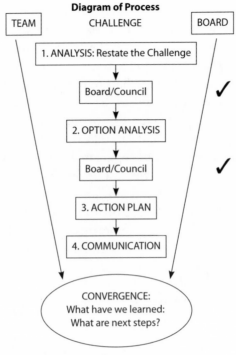

Figure 15

- The team then works with the challenge through a process of questions and research. After several weeks the team might discover that the challenge or experiment they have been given needs to be restated or given a different shape than originally conceived. This is quite normal and is part of the process of learning to do adaptive work.
- The team meets again with the board to share the work it has done and any adaptations it proposes to meet the challenge it was given. In this dialogue the board members learn more about how to lead change as well as build their confidence that this is a process that continues to engage them more deeply. In this safe space they can continue to learn how mission innovation takes place.
- The team then goes away to work on some options they can use in putting the experiment into action.

178

- At the end of this time they meet again with the board to share what they have done and seek the permission of the board to move forward.
- The next stage is for the team to develop an action plan and a way to communicate it to the church.
- They meet again with the board and share their work. At this point the board confirms the work and the experiment is initiated.
- After a period of time the board and team meet together to assess what has happened and what they have learned about experimenting and innovating missional life. On the basis of this evaluation, the board usually becomes very committed to the process and begins to plan new experiments.

15

The Experiment Stage

Little Steps toward Something Big

An artist once tried to build a pyramid on a seashore out of the rocks that lay about on the beach. He filmed his effort in order to record it as part of his artistic work. As the camera rolled, one could see the artist carefully placing one rock upon another. They would totter and then fall to the ground. Each time he began again with the same rocks, and each time the pyramid grew a little higher. This went on for several hours as the tide came in around the artist. Finally, he stood before the camera and said: "Each time I take a rock and add it to the pile, the pyramid grows higher. Each time the rocks fall down, I get to know them a little better and am able to place them in ways that cause the pyramid to grow." Each time he placed a rock, it was an experiment that allowed him to learn how to build the pyramid.

An experiment is a course of action that a group tentatively adopts without knowing exactly what the experiments will produce. It allows new concepts to be tried without requiring complete commitment. In this stage of the process groups get to test new ideas about what it means to be missional. As more and more people become involved in such experiments, the social system begins to shift to reflect a congregation that is living missionally. Instead of implementing a large program or organizational change to move a church toward missional life, cultivating small experiments allows missional life to arise from the grass roots and thereby lead to long-term change.

Why experiments? The simple answer is that they give people permission to fail. Why is this so important? It seems counterintuitive—surely you want people to succeed, not fail. Yes! But by giving permission to fail, we cultivate a context in which people feel safe to risk initiating simple experiments in missional life in which they can succeed. All of this is vitally important for the innovation of missional life from among the people.

Alan recently led a weekend workshop for a mainline denomination's mission planning committee. After listening to Alan describe ways of engaging the neighborhood and practicing hospitality to those in their communities, one of the leaders of the committee confided that this was going to be a major shift in their way of thinking and operating as churches. He went on to say that he and his wife would have a very hard time with this way of being the church because they had no experience in connecting outside their church circles. Inviting the neighbors over for dinner (a simple experiment in missional life) felt like trying to climb Mount Everest.

To gently invite people into this kind of change, we need processes that give them permission to try and fail, because that is the only way any of us ever really learns to develop new habits and skills. Alan's eighteen-month-old granddaughter, Madeline, is precocious and full of energy. She goes at life full bore. So these days when Alan sees Madeline, she often has bruises up and down her face. These are from learning not just to walk but to climb big obstacles, dance in front of everybody, and run after her brothers to try to catch up with them. These bruises are the signs of her experimenting. Of course we want to protect her, but we all recognize that without the testing and trying Madeline can never grow and move into the new stages of life. She needs to try and fail in order to adapt to her changing body and this amazing move from baby into childhood. It's the same with each of us when it comes to learning new habits. If inviting a neighbor over for dinner feels like a big risk, if we hardly know what is happening to folks next door, then we need to create an environment for experimenting in a way that gives us permission to fail. This is the way we learn new habits as well as discover that most of the time what we fear most actually doesn't happen.

Experiment Aversion

Within most churches we have managed to create a risk-aversive culture, which means that we are plagued by a condition we call *experiment aversion*. To counteract this, we have to find ways of gently inviting people into some low-level risks in order for them to learn new ways of being the church.

Several of the reasons for this risk-averse environment are important to mention since they are deeply shaping our imaginations, causing people to opt for safe, predictable, manageable outcomes. In the first place, some of the theologies we take for granted contribute to this environment. In the North American church, especially in its evangelical and restorational expressions, theologies of conversation carry with them the implications of perfectionism (what is sometimes understood as sanctification) that shuts down risk. The way these notions of conversion and Christian development have been interpreted is that once a person makes a personal commitment to Jesus Christ, he or she must live up to a perfectionistic standard. The church becomes an environment in which people have become risk-averse and the language of failure is not permitted (except as a concept we can all assent to as real, but not as a fact of our own corporate lives). The reality is that our transformation is much more like a long journey in the same direction in which we are continually living with the grace of God and the reality of humanity.

A second reason why churches have become risk-averse cultures is the overarching reality of professionalism that pervades most churches. Despite all the proclamation of the liberation of the laity, an inappropriate clericalism communicates that these *professionals* (clergy) are about the only ones who have control and knowledge over the *mysteries* of what God is up to in the church and in the world. Within this kind of environment, few are willing to risk and imagine experiments.

Finally, church systems are generally shaped by what we call *performative* leadership skills.[1] This means that most clergy and people

183

on church boards are in their positions because of demonstrated abilities in managing the existing paradigms of church life. In other words, they are skilled at leading on the basis of past performance. They know how things have been done but have little sense of what alternatives might be open to them. Furthermore, one of the important values guiding the performative leaders is that they don't want to create a mess or misguide the church on their watch. This makes such people inherently conservative and risk-resistant. These kinds of leaders may understand the need for missional transformation; they may even attend conferences or read books about the nature and meaning of missional transformation. The reality, however, is that they know performative leadership and have little sense of how to lead their communities into a different, adaptive way of engaging missional life. These are people who care deeply for their people. They feel responsible as leaders, but they don't want to be put in positions of being shamed by trying to lead their church into places it has never been before when they have no idea what that might mean.

For these reasons and many more, the anxiety that comes with risking new ventures and change must be respected. The language of experiments provides a means for doing this. What experiments say to people is that there are not going to be any big programs or major changes. In fact, almost everything will stay the same, which produces an environment of security. The experiments are small ways of addressing the question of forming mission-shaped life in the neighborhoods where we live. They might succeed, but they might not. The important thing is that only through such trying, testing, and experimenting do we learn new skills and habits.

Experimenting into Change

The innovation of mission-shaped life in a church has to involve a broad cross section of the church if it is to actually enter the congregation's DNA. There are so many illustrations of great ideas, plans, ideals, and formulas for creating mission-shaped life that flourish for a brief time only to quickly fade or die out once the creative or charismatic pastor moves on. The process of experimenting is a

184

way of moving past these episodic activities to transform the DNA toward continuing missional life. Experiments assist a congregation in learning its way into a new approach to being church together.

The power of experiments is that they don't require the whole church to do something all at once. Most people in a healthy church (70 to 75 percent) are comprised of what we call the *broad middle*— they are relatively okay with the church at the moment. There are things they would change if they had the choice, but they don't want to cause conflict and really don't have a sense of what the options might be. This broad middle will continue to default to its professional leaders and opt for the status quo so long as things seem to be moving along without too much conflict. These people will not lead a charge into adaptive change or mission-shaped life. They will vote for, or even join, the mission project in the community or across the country (e.g., building with Habitat for Humanity or short-term volunteering somewhere), but these actions don't change the culture of a church or form an ongoing mission-shaped life within neighborhoods and communities. We cannot expect this kind of transformation to come from these people. This is not blame or criticism; it's not even a comment on some kind of low-level spiritual commitment. This is just how we work as human beings.

At the same time, a relatively healthy local church will also have a small percentage of people who are eager and energized to experiment. These are the early adopters that we mentioned in the last chapter, and usually they comprise 10 to 15 percent of the church. This is the group out of which are selected the people to work with the experiments identified by the church board. These early adopters turn the board challenge into an experiment and then meet with the board at regular intervals to report and dialogue with them about what is happening.

Once other people in the church observe some successful results from the early experiments, they start believing that they too can participate in an experiment. The idea is that a few people in the church carry out the initial set of experiments, and then others are given the ability to see how they themselves can do something similar in their contexts. In this way a growing number of people slowly start to learn new habits and skills of being God's missionary people in their neighborhoods.

[handwritten margin note: Who are these in your church?]

185

A key element of this experiment process is the understanding it produces of how missional change takes place. As we have indicated already, this kind of change does not come through large programs, whole systems change, or top-down vision, mission, and strategic plans. It comes about as small groups of people in a local community learn to enter small experiments of mission in their neighborhoods (such as the practice of hospitality). What we have learned is that to transform the DNA of a local church from being primarily attractional to becoming missional doesn't require everyone being involved. Once around 20 percent of a local church is entering into missional experiments, the system shifts and won't go back.

Leaving structures and organizational life basically in place creates the requisite context of predictability and security from which the experiments can be initiated. If we force experiments and change structures, the result is almost always increasing resistance. People focus on the structure and organizational change, and it becomes the focus of anxiety and resistance to the extent that the experiments become associated with disruption and reaction. By leaving the structure and organization untouched, an environment of security supports the development of experiments. They are seen, at first, as interesting actions that can be noted. As they grow, however, they gradually draw others into new processes of experimentation in mission-shaped life. The broad middle slowly comes to see that these movements of mission into the neighborhood are giving new energy and life to the church. As this takes place (it will require several years rather than months), people will gradually come to see the need to change structures and programs to support the new forms of missional life that have sprung up across the church. Organizational and structural change follow a missional transformation process even though it could not have been lead into it.

Experimenting with Getting to Know

Through the process of listening to the reports from the dialogue groups, many different experiments will come forth. It is amazing how creative people can be when they are given the freedom to explore the possibilities. Following we provide some concrete examples of the experiment of *getting to know one's neighbors* that can help mobilize churches to engage their neighborhoods.

It is fascinating how those most involved in church life have the least time to engage their neighbors with simple conversation. Recently a group of pastors were asked to enter their own neighborhoods and get to know those who lived in the area. One pastor, who had lived in his community for about ten years, wrote to say that he didn't know where to start, so he got some members of his church who lived close by to introduce him to people in the neighborhood. He then reported this story: As he began to enter his neighborhood, he found out that the older couple next door had been there when he and his family arrived almost a decade earlier. He discovered that the husband had died about three months earlier, and now his neighbor was a widow struggling to make it on her own. This opened the door for conversations about her needs and how those in the immediate neighborhood could serve her.

There is something crucial to keep in mind with this experiment: The group of people who are empowered by the board to do a *getting to know* experiment must realize that they are to simply get to know people and listen to them. They are not to go out with their Bible up their sleeve, waiting for an opportunity to proselytize. Engaging neighbors with this experiment means that people simply become present in their neighborhoods and begin to engage people in natural ways of friendship.

In another city a teenager had spent most of his Sundays skateboarding around a church during their services. Later, in his twenties and thirties, he became a victim of alcoholism to the point that he and his wife were in need of help to survive. Another church in the area was working through the questions of how it could experiment in missional life, and they knew it meant testing and experimenting by moving back into the neighborhood. Some of the church members who lived only a few streets apart decided their experiment would involve getting to know their neighbors, starting with some street barbeques in the summer and inviting folks over to their homes for supper. They ran into the alcoholic couple—the man who had once skateboarded madly around the church on Sundays. This couple was taken in and loved deeply by the church members right on the

187

street where they lived. Since this couple never would have crossed the boundary into a church, a house church experiment was begun in that neighborhood.

From that simple experiment emerged the sense that the Spirit wanted to do something new in that city. As a result a series of neighborhood house churches were started, and Christians living in the same community came together to ask how they could practice hospitality to their neighbors without requiring that they drive twenty minutes to their churches. A new imagination for church in this new space is now being birthed. It could only have come out of people being ready to risk and experiment when they didn't know where it would all go.

The Experiment of Hospitality

An experiment that is powerful for seeing what God is up to in the neighborhoods is to practice hospitality with neighbors. *Hospitality* is a central practice highlighted in the Scriptures; it is about embracing the stranger—the one who thinks differently. Often hospitality has been relegated in the church to something good cooks do after Sunday evening church services. But the act of hospitality is not something that only applies to those who like to cook.

Hospitality is about making room in our lives and in the personal space of our homes for those we classify as strangers. To do this we need to create an experiment in which a group of people are empowered and supported in the endeavor of inviting neighbors into their homes for dinner. The group might establish a goal of doing this at least once a month. These acts of hospitality can potentially lead to conversations about life, opinions, and how they view this walk in the current clearing. People outside the church are feeling stress as they experience radical and unpredictable change, and few have a place where it is safe to share their *clearing* experience.

At first neighbors might be skeptical about an invitation to your home. Some have been used in such settings, so they may think that you will spring a multilevel marketing scheme on them. But as friendship develops, it will become more natural to invite them to a simple meal and engage them in sharing a little bit of life together.

To help a group do the hospitality experiment, it is essential to allow the Scripture to shape the imagination of the group. It is not enough to simply go and do it. This might result in some good actions, but we are looking for more than actions. We are looking to have our inner being reshaped so that the actions become a part of who we are. Therefore, reflecting on a passage of Scripture as a group is vital to this process. Luke 10:1–12 has proven to be especially valuable in our work with church.

> After this the Lord appointed seventy-two others and sent them two by two ahead of him to every town and place where he was about to go. He told them, "The harvest is plentiful, but the workers are few. Ask the Lord of the harvest, therefore, to send out workers into his harvest field. Go! I am sending you out like lambs among wolves. Do not take a purse or bag or sandals; and do not greet anyone on the road.
>
> "When you enter a house, first say, 'Peace to this house.' If a man of peace is there, your peace will rest on him; if not, it will return to you. Stay in that house, eating and drinking whatever they give you, for the worker deserves his wages. Do not move around from house to house.
>
> "When you enter a town and are welcomed, eat what is set before you. Heal the sick who are there and tell them, 'The kingdom of God is near you.' But when you enter a town and are not welcomed, go into its streets and say, 'Even the dust of your town that sticks to our feet we wipe off against you. Yet be sure of this: The kingdom of God is near.' I tell you, it will be more bearable on that day for Sodom than for that town."

We have a thirteen-week hospitality group process.[2] During these weeks a group learns the discipline of "Dwelling in the Word," reading Luke 10 each time they gather and listening to what God might be saying to them about practicing hospitality in their neighborhoods. When we lead this process it's always refreshing to see how something new shapes people's imagination for missional engagement in their communities.

189

Within this process, a group experiments with cooking meals and sharing them with others in the neighborhood then learning to ask new questions about what they think God may be up to in the neighborhood and how they can join with God in these things. It all sounds simple, but often the simplest things are the most important.

Conclusion

Commitment

A few years ago, a medium-sized, successful attractional church in Anchorage, Alaska, realized that while they were one of the more effective churches in town, they were not doing what God had called them to do. They wanted more than more noses to count on Sundays. They entered a time of reflection and research, seeking to discern what they might do. The result was a season of transition, involving listening and becoming aware of their own stories and the people of their communities. This created space for people to evaluate what was going on in their church, and from this they began experiments where they engaged their communities. Over time, this process led the church to commit itself to a new path.

In one experiment a group was practicing hospitality. As they related to people in their neighborhoods, some got to know a single mom who had all kinds of questions about life, her struggles as a parent, and what God had to do with the tough knocks she had experienced. She began to join people in the group for meals on a regular basis, becoming part of the rhythm of their lives. As conversations over meals began to reshape her imagination, she discovered a community of people who cared for her. In time she embraced Jesus. But something started to happen to the group as well. They were learning that God was up to and involved in the lives of a lot of people in their neighborhood even if these people didn't attend a church or call themselves Christians. What they were discovering was that by creating a table (food and conversation) and making it a safe space (not about manipulating people or getting them to become something), they became aware of a dynamic of the Spirit none of them had ever imagined. It was amazing what was happening in the neighborhood. They had always been so busy trying to get people to go to church that they had never had their eyes opened to what God was up to in the most unlikely people. As the months went by, they began to sense a new way of being God's people out in the neighborhood.

Over the next couple of years, the single mother moved closer to others in the group to share a sense of community, and to get out of an impoverished situation. She matured in the Lord through the relationships that she had built over meals. Her kids became part of a larger family and felt a sense of security.

As the church continued to experiment with the call of mission, more people in church became committed to living missionally. The young single mother was challenged with the fact that many of her friends from her old neighborhood were stuck in a destructive way of life from which they could not break free. She came to her new church community, entering a conversation about her own awareness of these friends and their challenges. Together they sought to understand the situation and what God was saying.

Unbelievably, these conversations resulted in something no one could have planned or imagined: she moved back into the old neighborhood to live again among neighbors in need. Her church community, working with Habitat for Humanity, built her a home. She is a seamstress, so she began making clothes and selling them. In ways she would never have imagined just a year earlier, her little business began to grow. She hired some of her old friends, most of whom were single mothers. As they worked side by side, all kinds of conversations started to happen about life and God because the gospel was no longer an abstract idea; it became real through the living presence of a single mom who took a chance on moving back into her neighborhood in the name of Jesus. This missional experiment led to some radical commitments on the part of these women. They set up five different communities meeting in homes. This simple seamstress shop owner became a volunteer pastor among these community-based groups of single mothers. The Good News of the gospel came to life as the church became a sign, foretaste, and witness to God's dream for the world.

Missional Engagement

This is a story of missional engagement. It illustrates something more than personal salvation or church attendance. This woman entered a community of Christians struggling to become aware of what was going on in their world by moving back into their own neighborhoods. They entered into conversation and listened to each other so that they might understand and evaluate options. Then they experimented. All of this led to commitment to a very specific way of missional engagement.

Such stories are exhilarating and motivating. To hear this story and try to replicate it fails to realize it's not about copying but participating in a process. But there is something within all of us that wants to leap into the tangible results of commitment—the last stage of the Missional Change Model—without walking through the process that will actually produce commitment. Good intentions, and lots of theoretical understanding of what commitment looks like, won't take a church community into this kind of missional engagement. It's about learning how to begin this kind of listening, discerning, experimenting journey in your own context.

This journey toward missional commitment will take time. It doesn't happen overnight. It will take a local church five to six years to make this transition. But when a church enters into the commitment stage, people look back over the journey to see they've taken on new habits, practices, and values. This is the point when people start talking about how they might change structures, roles, organization, and programs to reflect the new place where they find themselves.

As a church moves through the Missional Change Model for the first time, there will be an initial group of early adopters (experimenters) who move through the process with energy and eagerness. They start to move toward the commitment stage in the first eighteen to twenty-four months. But remember this is only about 10 percent of a church; it's the beginning of the journey. Others will watch the early adopters, and some will want to join them in the process. In this way, more and more people are gently invited into the journey. We find that after the initial eighteen months, people are starting to "get" the process and the journey. They are experiencing some "early wins" and the church board is ready to ask how the Spirit is leading them to continue the process of adopting the Missional Change Model as part of their lives. After eighteen to twenty-four months, therefore, there will be an initial level of commitment to the missional journey and more people who desire to enter the process of the Missional Change Model by initiating new rounds of awareness, understanding, evaluation, and experimenting.

The journey toward commitment is not one of a leap across the great gulf but of a series of circling rounds. In the first round, the early adopters (maybe 10 percent) will venture out, but this does not mean the entire church is committed to the missional journey at this point. Instead, this first group is learning to catch the spirit of what is happening. They are learning to build a bridge across this vast gulf between what the church has been and the missional call. The Missional Change Model is, then, like a process for "building a bridge as we walk on it." It is not a predetermined bridge that we have sought to give you, a one-size-fits-all template that looks the same in all situations. It's a process that teaches us to build our own bridges in our own local contexts.

Deciding for More

As we introduced in chapter 14, the church board will have the responsibility of interacting with the teams doing the experiments. These teams will provide reports and share what they learned. Then the board must determine the next steps. They will identify new experiments, how new people can get involved in these experiments, and who will be involved with them.

Then after two or three rounds of walking people through the Missional Change Model, the board must determine how the life of missional engagement will impact the structure, staff, budget, and other organizational issues. This is the point when the church is moving into a greater and fuller sense of commitment.

The aim of part 3 of this book has been to assist you in doing the one important thing: beginning the journey of entering into the missional river of mystery, memory, and mission that we introduced in part 1 of this book. The Missional Change Model and the steps that we outlined in the last few chapters are ways to help you "get your feet wet" and begin sailing in the right direction. We've not given you all the details, nor laid out a plan for the next five years of your church's life. That would only result in a book too long to be helpful. We have other resources to help with that. This book is simply aimed at helping you get started.

A Parable

We want to end this book with a modern parable that is a true story about things that are happening today in America. Reflecting on how to capture what we have been saying, we saw a news report that is not directly about missional change and yet expresses so wonderfully the themes we have developed. The video report is about how people are coping with the economic crisis that is causing so much disruption and harm to thousands upon thousands of people across the continent.[1]

Correspondent John Larson talks with students in a high school in Pomona, California—one of the hardest hit areas in America for job loss and housing foreclosures. It is a story about kids and parents finding themselves in a new space where their maps of the American Dream are being torn up before their eyes. These are people who find themselves in a place of hopelessness where there seems to be few options.

The report was instigated by an assignment Michael Steinman gave his AP Literature class. In a very real way, he knows the plight of people in the community and the longings of his students to go to college and gain their part of the American Dream. In an entirely different way, however, he does not understand what is happening to his students. He teaches literature using *The Great Gatsby* as the text for talking about the American Dream. But Steinman says that when he asked the students about their stories, they came alive in ways he was not prepared for. He gave his students an assignment to write an anonymous essay about what the economy was doing to their families. These essays took his breath away. He was not prepared for the pain he read in these real, offstage stories of what was happening in the lives of his students and their families. He read about his students' deeply painful experiences in ways *The Great Gatsby* never could have called forth. These were the voices of his students, and through their stories the true picture developed of what was happening off the stage of formal classes and learning programs.

Steinman was so struck by what was happening in the lives of the kids in his class that he was moved to make them an offer. If they were willing to tell their stories on film, he would make sure the movie got to the presidential candidates. So these young people began to tell their own stories on a classroom video—ordinary kids were empowered to give voice to their stories, and in so doing, things began to happen. It wasn't that their worlds were suddenly changed like a happily-ever-after fairy tale, but they began to sense a new kind of empowerment and hope. These high school kids started to see that others were indeed listening and that it was possible to create a different space from the ground up in the midst of really tough times.

Watch their report on YouTube.[2] It is not a church story, but it is a core missional parable connecting many of the dots and themes we have sought to develop in this book. It shows us how we too can build a bridge as we walk on it. And as we do, we discover a new reality, one that is much more than missional church. We discover that we are living missionally.

Notes

Introduction

1. Lois Barrett, Inagrace T. Dietterich, Darrel L. Guder, George R. Hunsberger, Alan J. Roxburgh, and Craig Van Gelder, *Missional Church: A Vision for the Sending of the Church in North America*, ed. Darrel L. Guder (Grand Rapids: Eerdmans, 1998).

Chapter 1 Not All Who Wander Are Lost

1. Quoted in Stephen B. Bevans and Roger P. Schroeder, *Constants in Context: A Theology of Mission for Today* (Maryknoll, NY: Orbis, 2005), 309–10.

Chapter 2 Just Give Me a Definition

1. These texts include Isaiah 35:3–5, 61:1–2; Jeremiah 31:31–34; Mark 1:14–15, Mark 4:26–34; Matthew 13:44–52.

2. Walter Brueggemann, *Deep Memory, Exuberant Hope* (Minneapolis: Fortress, 2000), 3.

3. Ibid., 4.

4. See Lesslie Newbigin, *The Open Secret: An Introduction to the Theology of Mission* (Grand Rapids: Eerdmans, 1995), 5. Leaders who want to further develop these themes of the church as mission would be well served by a study of this little book. While it may not be the kind of text with which to initiate the missional conversation in a congregation new to these ideas, the book easily lends itself to being designed as a series of Bible studies that would make a powerful resource for shaping missional understanding in the church. This kind of resource could be turned into an ongoing training class used for the introduction and initiation of people into the life, ministry, and leadership of the church. No one should be giving leadership in the church without first living deeply into the memory of the narratives so splendidly presented by Newbigin in this volume.

Chapter 3 Does *Missional* Fit?

1. See Rodney Stark, *What Americans Really Believe* (Waco: Baylor University Press, 1998).

2. Chris Erdman, *Countdown to Sunday: A Daily Guide for Those Who Dare to Preach* (Grand Rapids: Brazos, 2007).

3. For more information, go to http://www.the-landing.org/main.cfm.

4. Richard Dawkins, *The God Delusion* (Boston: Houghton Mifflin, 2006); Christopher Hitchens, *God Is Not Great: How Religion Poisons Everything* (New York: Twelve, 2007).

5. The 1990 edition of the *Concise Oxford Dictionary* defines nostalgia as (1) a sentimental yearning for a period of the past, (2) regretful or wistful memory of an earlier time, (3) severe homesickness.

Chapter 5 We're Not in Kansas Anymore

1. This chapter is a thoroughly revised and updated version of a chapter that first appeared in Alan Roxburgh, *Reaching a New Generation* (Downers Grove, IL: InterVarsity, 1993).

2. Charles Taylor, *A Secular Age* (Cambridge, MA: Belknap, 2007), 143.

3. These reflections on place and space are dependent upon the important work done by Walter Brueggemann in his book *The Land: Place as Gift, Promise and Challenge in Biblical Faith*, 2nd ed. (Minneapolis: Fortress, 2002), 3–5.

4. Stanley Hauerwas and William Willimon, *Resident Aliens* (Nashville: Abingdon, 1989), 15–17.

5. John W. de Gruchy, *Theology and Ministry in Context and Crisis: A South African Perspective* (London: Collins, 1986), 158.

6. See David Watson, *I Believe in the Church* (Grand Rapids: Eerdmans, 1978).

7. See, for example, Ebbie Smith, *Growing Healthy Congregations: New Directions for Church Growth in the 21st Century* (Ft. Worth: Church Starting Network, 2003), and Christian Schwarz, *Natural Church Development* (St. Charles, IL: Church Smart Resources, 1996).

8. Information about Fresh Expressions can be found at http://www.freshexpressions.org.uk/index.asp?id=1.

Chapter 6 Why Do We Need Theology?

1. Robert J. Schreiter, *Constructing Local Theologies* (Maryknoll, NY: Orbis, 1985).

2. Ibid., 16.

3. Clemens Sedmak, *Doing Local Theology: A Guide for Artisans of a New Humanity* (Maryknoll, NY: Orbis, 2002), 3.

4. A great book that shows how this happens in another of Paul's letters is Brian J. Walsh and Sylvia C. Keesmaat, *Colossians Remixed: Subverting the Empire* (Downers Grove, IL: InterVarsity, 2004).

Chapter 7 God's Dream for the World

1. Gerhard Lohfink, *Jesus and Community*, trans. Herder Verlag (Minneapolis: Fortress, 1984), 28.

2. Barry Harvey, *Can These Bones Live? A Catholic Baptist Engagement with Ecclesiology, Hermeneutics, and Social Theory* (Grand Rapids: Brazos, 2008).

Chapter 8 The Journey Ahead

1. See Walter Brueggemann, *The Land: Place as Gift, Promise, and Challenge in Biblical Faith*, 2nd ed. (Minneapolis: Fortress Press, 2002).

Chapter 10 The Missional Change Model

1. See Alan Roxburgh, *The Sky Is Falling: Leaders Lost in Transition* (Eagle, ID: Allelon, 2007).

2. For a detailed description of the leadership functions, see Alan Roxburgh and Fred Romanuk, *The Missional Leader: Equipping Your Church to Reach a Changing World* (San Francisco: Jossey-Bass, 2007).

3. Peter Block, *Community: The Structure of Belonging* (San Francisco: Barrett-Koehler, 2008), 85.

4. Ibid., 88.

Chapter 11 The Awareness Stage

1. Mark Lau Branson, *Memories, Hopes and Conversations: Appreciative Inquiry and Congregational Change* (New York: Alban, 2006).

2. Available at www.roxburghmissionalnet.com.

Chapter 14 The Work of the Church Board

1. For further information, go to www.roxburghmissionalnet.com.

2. Available at www.roxburghmissionalnet.com.

3. The details of the retreat are in the *Mission-Shaped Church Field Guide*, which is available at www.roxburghmissionalnet.com.

4. The details of this process are in the *Mission-Shaped Church Field Guide* (see n. 33). We are simply summarizing here the overall work of the board and the teams. Remember that this is a discussion about initiating the learning process for innovating missional life, so our focus here is on how the board learns and gets inside this part of the process at the beginning.

Chapter 15 The Experiment Stage

1. See Roxburgh and Romanuk, *Missional Leader*, for a detailed description of performative leadership.

2. See www.roxburghmissionalnet.com for this hospitality Bible study.

Conclusion: Commitment

1. John Larson, "Is Anybody Listening?" produced by Karen Foshay, ed. Alberto Arce, Michael Bloecher, and "Lil" Joe Whiting, *KCET Local*, March 19, 2009, http://kcet.org/socal/2009/03/is-anybody-listening.html.

2. http://kcet.org/socal/2009/03/is-anybody-listening---where-it-all-began.html.

Alan J. Roxburgh is a teacher, trainer, and consultant who works with Allelon and internationally framing resources for the missional church. He coordinates an international project involving leaders from twelve nations who are examining leadership formation in a globalized world. He is the author or coauthor of several books, including *The Missional Church*, *The Missional Leader and Leadership*, *Liminality and the Missionary Congregation*, and *Reaching a New Generation*. He and his wife Jane live in Vancouver, Canada, and have three grown children.

M. Scott Boren is one of the pastors at Woodland Hills Church in St. Paul, Minnesota. He is a trainer, consultant, and the author of *The Relational Way* and *How Do We Get There From Here?* He works with Allelon in developing training materials on the missional church. He shares life with his wife Shawna and their four children.

ALLELON
A Movement of Missional Leaders

Allelon's mission is to **educate** and **encourage** the church to become a people among whom God can live, as sign, symbol, and foretaste of his redeeming love and grace in their neighborhoods and the whole of society—ordinary women and men endeavoring to participate in God's mission to reclaim and restore the whole of creation and to bear witness to the world of a new way of being human.

Visit **www.allelon.org** to read current missional thinkers, learn about our projects and resources, and more.

- Video and Audio of Leading Missional Thinkers and Practitioners
- Articles and Conversations
- Allelon Training Centers
- International Research Project: Mission in Western Culture

The word *allelon* is a common but overlooked New Testament word that is reciprocal in nature. Christian faith is not an individual matter. Everything in the life of the church is done *allelon*, for the sake of the world. A Christian community is defined by the *allelon* sayings in Scripture. We are to love one another. We are to pursue one another's good. We are to build up one another. We are to bear with one another in love. We are to bear one another's burdens. We are to be kind to one another. We are to be compassionate to one another. We are to be forgiving to one another. We are to submit to one another. We are to consider one another better than ourselves. We are to be devoted to one another in love. We are to live in harmony with one another.

Roxburgh Missional Network
catalyst for missional transformation

360s

Workshops

Webinars

Training

Coaching

Blog/Articles

How we address the issues of being the church today in the midst of huge culture change will shape us tomorrow. Becoming vital centers of mission in our communities no longer depends on categories we've taken for granted. The best practices of contemporary church life will no longer prepare us for the levels of change we face—we live in an *age of the unthinkable.*

The future of the church will depend on cultivating, discerning, and calling forth the unthinkable among the people of God in ordinary local churches.

Roxburgh Missional Network is a team of missional practitioners committed to partnering with you in forming leaders and churches that are vital centers of mission. We provide real-time, **concrete, hands-on resources** and **tools** that give pastors, denominational leaders, and congregations the capacities to address their challenges in forming mission-shaped communities. Our road-tested tools and resources are effective and cultivate mission-shaped transformation.